More praise for

SETTLING IN

"Richard Morgan has a passion for enhancing the lives of older adults. Upon reading his latest book, my desire is to share it with others, for it is comprehensive and 'rings true.' He speaks of his own insightful experiences in making the transition to retirement community living, with all the accompanying challenges and joys. Dr. Morgan's narrative offers encouragement and support to those who are making this journey."

—James D. Ludwick
Chaplain/Pastor
Otterbein-Lebanon Retirement Living Community
and United Methodist Church

"*Settling In* captures well the wide range of emotions typically experienced by residents in their initial years in a continuing care retirement community. The author conceals few of his feelings and criticisms, candidly describing the difficulties in the transition from a home and lifestyle of many years to a congregate care environment. Morgan's deep and pervasive theological grounding and pastoral commitment gives the book a meditative character with each of the fifty-two vignettes beginning with thoughtfully selected scripture and ending with prayer."

—Samuel M. Stone
Executive Director
Glenaire Continuing Care Retirement Community

SETTLING IN

MY FIRST YEAR *in a* RETIREMENT COMMUNITY

RICHARD L. MORGAN

UPPER ROOM BOOKS®
NASHVILLE

SETTLING IN
MY FIRST YEAR IN A RETIREMENT COMMUNITY
© 2006 by Richard L. Morgan
All rights reserved.

The Upper Room Web Site: http://www.upperroom.org

At the time of publication all Web sites referenced in this book were valid. However, due to the fluid nature of the internet some addresses may have changed or the content may no longer be relevant.

Scripture quotations not otherwise identified are from the New Revised Standard Version of the Bible, © 1989 by the Division of Christian Education of the National Council of the Churches of Christ in the USA. Used by permission. All rights reserved.

Page 190 serves as an extension of this copyright page.

Cover design: John Hamilton Design
Cover photo: Photodisc
First printing: 2006

LIBRARY OF CONGRESS CATALOGING-IN-PUBLICATION
Morgan, Richard Lyon, 1929–
  Settling in: my first year in a retirement community / Richard L. Morgan
     p. cm.
  Includes index.
  ISBN-13: 978-0-8358-9908-6
  ISBN-10: 0-8358-9908-X
  1. Retirees—Prayer-books and devotions—English. 2. Older people—Prayer-books and devotions—English. 3. Aging—Religious aspects—Christianity—Meditations. 4. Older Christians—Religious life. 5. Retirement—Religious aspects—Christianity. 6. Morgan, Richard Lyon, 1929– I. Title.
  BV4596.R47M67 2007
  248.8'5—dc22
                                    2006023037

Printed in the United States of America

To the residents and staff at
Redstone/North Huntingdon

WHOSE AUTHENTICITY AND CARE
DEMONSTRATE WHAT A
BLESSED COMMUNITY
CAN BE.

CONTENTS

〰

FOREWORD

In laying bare his soul in *Settling In*, Dick Morgan has created a way for us not-yet-frail older adults, for those who serve elders, and for family members of elders facing life in a retirement community to face our own fears of what it might be like to live in a "place like that." He also offers elders who are already living in such settings an authentic way to reflect on their experience from a spiritual perspective— a refreshing challenge.

This is not a cheerleader's guide to long-term care. Rather, it is the story of intense pilgrimage, of quest for the presence and call of God in this new situation, this new lifestyle. It reflects the roller-coaster ride the first year in such a strange and confining institution can be.

Chapter by chapter, from the time of contemplating the move to having lived there for a year, Morgan takes us deeper and deeper into his lived experience and does not whitewash it a bit. He shares his initial excitement in the newness of the move, then reflects on the realities of life with other elders, many of whom are much older than he. He speaks of the loss of his former status as a well-known pastor in a lovely North Carolina community, loss that is countered by the joy of new physical and emotional proximity to family, especially grandchildren.

Morgan speaks frankly of his struggle with depression; of attempts to find his own niche, to create Christian community;

and of his special love for those most likely to be excluded from community—those with dementia. He also describes some hilarious situations that occur!

My fears of life in the fourth quarter (after seventy-five) are not particular to me. In general, three major fears hinder older adults' enjoyment of and full engagement in our years after sixty-five:

1. a loss of health, which robs us of energy and renders us functionally disabled and/or in pain, often dependent on others' help;

2. a loss of cognitive ability and short-term memory, which renders us increasingly unable to engage with others on an intellectually equal playing field, and;

3. a loss of social status, which makes us feel unwanted and unneeded, extra baggage in an already financially strained economy.

Perhaps the greatest fear of all is that, because the above events occur, we may be forced—against our desire, counter to our preference—to live in a "retirement community."

Because of this predominant, overwhelming, looming fear, older adult advocacy groups and service planners (many of whom are baby boomers or younger) are currently focusing on helping older adults to "age in place," offering a variety of services to allow them to stay at home as long as they desire. In many ways this is an ideal of the baby boom generation who can't imagine what life is like when one is too frail to change a lightbulb or get the rotting garbage out of the house.

A few people—most of them younger outsiders—have spoken of the retirement community experience. But few have spoken of it from the "inside," as a real-life resident, not a visitor, a service provider, or a researcher. The Reverend Richard Morgan has had the courage to do just that. He has broken the silence of what it is really like to live in such a place by examining and opening his own personal journal that describes his process of moving to and living in a continuing care retirement community.

Settling In is a book of hope and of the special vocation of the person who is called to the monastery of the long-term care facility. It speaks loudly of the continuing call of a God with hands outstretched, who is always challenging us to further horizons, larger concerns, and constantly surprising us with new ways to love and be loved.

JANE THIBAULT

Associate professor, Family and Geriatric Medicine
School of Geriatric Medicine, University of Louisville

PREFACE

At age seventy-four, I left my home in the state of North Carolina, which I dearly loved and where I had lived for fifty years, to come to a retirement community in Pennsylvania. In a real way, I left my identity, forged over years of hard work and experience, to start a new life as a relative nobody. At times I endured sleepless nights, worrying if I had made the right decision.

Although I had worked as a chaplain and volunteer in retirement communities and nursing homes, becoming a member of the community was a far different experience. Formerly I could walk out the front door of these communities and return to my home. I could push aside the sadness and struggles of older people and withdraw to the sanctuary of a warm home—but no longer. Now the retirement community became my home. Now every day I must confront the inevitable illnesses of old age as I walk the halls and talk with residents.

While I could not minimize the difficulties and issues I faced in this new lifestyle, *it gave me a view of this life as an insider*. As a resident I became a participant in this life, not an observer who only sees from the outside. I kept my credentials as a clergyperson and counselor, but before long my real identity had been linked with this community.

These meditations grew out of my journals that I wrote for a year. At times I wrote them in the quiet of my apartment;

at other times I would scribble notes on napkins, recording bits of conversation I heard in the dining room. In other settings I would try to recall experiences of working with people with Alzheimer's disease or other forms of dementia. All of these notes in my journal served to help me understand this new life experience.

Reflecting later on my experience, I discerned three major stages of this spiritual journey:

1. Initial excitement and euphoria, which lasts several weeks.

2. Second thoughts and regrets that plunged me into depression lasting several months.

3. A time of discernment about my life in this particular community, which took almost a year. I discovered a new ministry in this community; it began to feel like home.

At first, it was an exciting transition. Everything went exceptionally well. We sold our house in two days, and my wife engineered a smooth move, even though it meant downsizing two-thirds of our possessions. We loved the scenic beauty and new buildings of Redstone Highlands. Although it felt strange to live in an apartment, we adjusted and spent much of the summer exploring a new state and a new area. A new world awaited us. That sense of adventure didn't last very long. Soon regrets and second thoughts moved in.

I realized I had gilded the lily and relied on cognitive dissonance to make this place seem better than it was. Homesickness for my old community set in; everything seemed strange and unwelcome. My thoughts returned to the year 1997, when we made what I thought was our final move to a quaint little town called Morganton, North Carolina. This was to be our final "staying place," a town whose charm and gentle culture made it "Number Ten in the Nation" as a great place to raise a family or spend your retirement years. I remembered days and nights when I could greet friends on downtown streets. In Morganton I was known and recognized as an author, historian, and volunteer—I was "somebody." Now I was "nobody," a stranger in a strange place. There I had so many friends; here we only knew two adults and two children, our children and grandchildren.

After prayer and long conversations with God, I began to realize that my wife's and my willingness to uproot our lives and move here was a call from God, a way to live out our faith in our later years. One year later I would be nowhere else. There will always be twinges of nostalgia for the home we left. We miss our friends and the relationships that gave life meaning. But *this* village has become home. The residents here are my family, and a new ministry has made this a good place to be for the duration of my years.

Jane Thibault, an author who writes about later life, thinks that our later years can become a "natural monastery." She claims in the *Aging & Spirituality* newsletter that "in a very real sense, the experience of old age, especially frail elderhood, is an experience of living monastically." At first I scoffed at such a thought, but now I realize the truth of her words. It is here that we have pared down to the barest essentials; here that we have time for contemplation; here that we can become the blessed community, bound by love and prayer.

Perhaps you are considering a continuing care/retirement community when you retire. These meditations are for you. No one ever prepared me for this major late-life transition.

I hope that my experience will help you in your transition. Henry Simmons, who wrote the Introduction to this book, identifies three stable periods of aging in his book written with Jane Wilson *Soulful Aging: Ministries through the Stages of Adulthood*, each followed by a transition. I felt good in my Extended Middle Age; but I knew that the Ready or Not stage was just around the corner, since the farther one gets past age seventy-five the greater the possibility of frailty and major losses. I knew full well the day would come for my personal passage into dependence, the Like It or Not stage. I was ready to forge a new identity by living in a retirement community. It is a thin line between feeling not ready to enter a retirement community and the finality of it's too late and facing the grim reality of being taken where you do not want to go. How much better to own the decision and make your plans.

This book is also for adult children and caregivers who help older parents or relatives consider the possibility of a retirement home. This is a difficult time for families. It can create wounded feelings, heartbreak, and even broken relationships. As you seek to invite, counsel, and persuade your loved ones to consider this option, these meditations are for you. Perhaps it will smooth the rough places and make your task easier. Or, if you are a member of the dynamic baby boomer generation, who in a few years will retire and demand a quality of later life not offered in some communities, this book is for you. Perhaps you will learn from my experience and be pioneers of necessary changes in the continuing care/retirement community industry.

Finally, if you are a person who works in a retirement community, a person upon whom we depend for so much, this book is for you. As you read the first-year experience of this resident on the inside, you may better understand the struggles to make a place a home. We need your expertise and compassion to live here with joy and meaning.

For some time I had pestered my wife about moving to a retirement community, but I never thought it would happen so soon. The story of Abram and Sarai leaving their home in their later years intersected with our own. They had their struggles and conflicts, as have we. Yet God's promise to Abram and Sarai, "'I will bless you . . . so that you will be a blessing'" (Gen. 12:2), has become our promise too. God has blessed us here, and we seek to be a blessing to others. So I can attest that life in a retirement community can be the best years of your life. Now at long last, I begin to know what the poet meant,

> Grow old along with me!
> The best is yet to be,
> The last of life, for which the first was made:
> Our times are in his hand
> Who saith, "A whole I planned,
> Youth shows but half; trust God: see all, nor be afraid!"[1]

—RICHARD L. MORGAN
Redstone Highlands
North Huntingdon, Pennsylvania

Note: I wish to thank all of the residents of Redstone Highlands, North Huntingdon, who shared stories and experiences. The stories in this book are based on real people and situations in a retirement community, but names, in most cases, remain anonymous to protect their privacy.

INTRODUCTION
THE THIRD AGE

The years from fifty to death—the third age—are times of promise and of terror, of success and of failure, of grace and of sin. They are the best of times and the worst of times. They call forth the human person to growth and self-transcendence. Aging is a time of probable loss; it is also a time of possible gain.

On a human canvas of this breadth and intensity, Richard Morgan paints a picture of his life's journey in a retirement community. his word-picture lays out with passionate honesty four great life themes that recur with new urgency in the last third of life: freedom, intimacy, meaning, and death. These themes, which have been part of my thinking for twenty years, resonated with particular depth as I read Richard Morgan's manuscript.

Freedom. I contend that the human quest to be free, to be ourselves, to be unfettered, to speak forthrightly with our own voice becomes more an issue as we age than in the years when we are bound by the demands of the life of the house-holder: pleasing the boss, keeping a paycheck coming, gaining status and objects, "making it." This quest for voice might take the form of an insistence on choosing our own room-mate or table mate in a nursing home; it might lead into the thicket of choices about whom to support in a custody case when access to grandchildren is at stake; it might lead us to a new sense of self-direction in the use of time.

Clearly the old ways of making sense of the world of personal relationships needs the energy and integrity of freedom—freedom to tell the truth, to forgive ourselves and others, to blame and accuse, to uncover family myths, to claim our own fragile truth.

Intimacy. This is a lovely word; a fleshy, rooted, face-to-face word. Other words like *community, friendship, communion* may point to the same reality, but they do not capture the challenge of how intimacy shapes us when years are many. For some at the Morgans' new home, intimacy continues in the familiar ways of life together—sleeping, walking, eating, sharing, and loving. But this familiar intimacy is threatened by age, and a time of aloneness comes to most. For many, intimacy remains a struggle and a challenge—how to find and share the kinds of touch in love, in friendship, in words that bind person to person and make life human.

Meaning. "Without vision the people perish," we read in the Bible. That is true for the whole of human life. But the human need for meaning takes its own form in later life in mainstream American culture where old age is routinely seen as a time of retrogression, of failure, of decrepitude. In a world that views the normative human as young looking, productive, and physically well and active, the truest icon of age is the failing body. The first kind of meaning that we must seek in later life, then, is a personal resistance to the stereotypes of the culture. This must be supported in community.

We know people who succeed in making meaning, whose lives make sense to them, who waken each morning with a sense of giftedness, who find projects (inner and outer), tasks, and commitments that make sense of their days. At a more communal level, we see signs of promise in face-to-face groups where affirmations of worth are made by older adults to older adults that speak of a vision and lived reality that has little to do with cultural terrors of old age. These people and communities of meaning embody hope.

Death. Certainly we do not have to be old to die. But with the control of most infectious diseases, death is more likely to happen in old age and from degenerative disease. If we live long enough, we will likely die of failure of a major organ system. For some, this is a terrifying thought. For most, it is at least a sobering thought. If some fear death itself, others greatly fear not death but a long process of dying with chronic pain and loss of control.

These then are the great life themes that Richard Morgan speaks of in such real ways: freedom, intimacy, meaning, and death. This book testifies to its author's conviction that a sense of the sacred is the only adequate framework for discussing the promises and the challenges, as well as the ills and vagaries of age. This book gives flesh and blood, personality and color, passion and wit, candor and hope to this part of life's journey in one particular retirement home.

Dr. Henry S. Simmons
Director/Center on Aging
Union Theological Seminary
Richmond, Virginia

MAKING THE DECISION

Several Months

Life is a matter of beginnings and endings;
its rhythms ebb and flow.
But there is "music" in beginnings,
new energy and the creative
impulse to roam.[2]

—JOHN C. MORGAN

CONTINUING CARE
RETIREMENT COMMUNITIES

Continuing Care Retirement Communities usually have several levels of care in one setting. They may include:

Independent Living

Assisted Living for residents with mild to moderate Alzheimer's disease or dementia and persons with health issues who need personal care. (Some CCRCs now call Assisted Living *Personal Care.*)

Skilled Nursing or Health Care offers 24/7 skilled nursing care

Alzheimer's and Dementia Care provides required locked-down units for safety reasons. (Some CCRCs have special units called Memory Impairment.)

1 BEING PROACTIVE

Read Proverbs 6:6-10

Take a lesson from the ants, you lazybones.
Learn from their ways . . . they labor hard all summer,
gathering food for the winter.

PROVERBS 6:6-8 (NLT)

In Aesop's fable the ant worked assiduously through the oppressive summer heat to prepare for the harsh winter ahead. Meanwhile, the carefree grasshopper lounged in the shade, mocking the ant's relentless effort. He derided the ant for choosing labor over play; and when warned by the ant that winter was around the corner, the lazybones grasshopper scoffed and claimed there was plenty of time to prepare. In the end, the grasshopper waited too long and perished as a result of his procrastination. The writer of Proverbs counsels us, "Take a lesson from the ants. . . . They labor hard all summer, gathering food for the winter." What relevant advice for people in later life.

In an age when people live much longer and extend their years, how wise to plan for a metaphorical winter. People in the boomer generation, getting gray and facing retirement, also need to consider plans for home health care or investing in long-term care insurance or considering a retirement community with continuing care.

Read Luke 16:1-9. Jesus does not commend the manager for being dishonest but for foresight in planning for the future. The manager, knowing of his imminent dismissal, is concerned about what will happen to him and his family. So he devises a scheme to protect his future. By reducing some of the bills of his master's debtors, he incurs their gratitude and assures that he will be taken care of when he is out of a job. He looks ahead and plans for his future.

People in later life need to act resourcefully in their own interests, carefully planning for their future. Too many persons facing later life refuse to think about their future, let alone make plans. They push such thoughts out of their mind; and when that time comes, they find themselves unprepared. Their procrastination creates heavy burdens for family members who have to assume responsibility when the time comes. Some older parents feel that their children owe them and are to provide care for them when they can no longer stay in their homes. So adult children have to dance between guilt and anger, feeling the pain of guilt placed on them by their parents or anger that their parents did not make their own plans.

Years ago my wife and I decided to make plans for our later years. In so doing, we would own the decision and make this a gift to our children.

Loving God, we know you carry us even when we grow older and surround us with your grace. But you also expect us to take responsibility for our own lives. Grant us wisdom to make the right decision and courage to accept the consequences. Amen.

2 THE BARZILLAI SYNDROME REVISITED

Read 2 Samuel 19:31-39

Barzillai was a very aged man, eighty years old. . . . The king said to Barzillai, "Come over with me, and I will provide for you in Jerusalem at my side." But Barzillai said to the king, ". . . can I discern what is pleasant and what is not? Can your servant taste what he eats or what he drinks? Can I still listen to the voice of singing men and singing women? Why then should your servant be an added burden to my lord the king?"

2 SAMUEL 19:32–35

Barzillai didn't want to burden King David, even though David owed him a debt for his support in a moment of crisis. David offered him a pensioned place at his court for the rest of his days, promising him exquisite food, good wine, and all the comforts of a plush, retired life. But Barzillai cited many frailties of his age, including loss of his senses and faltering mental alertness. With these limitations he would need special care, which the king could not provide. After all, David had enough problems in his own family circle, without adding an aging friend. Barzillai chose to remain in his own land of Gilead and end his days amid known surroundings.

Sound familiar? It happens all the time. Older parents of the present generation have a different approach than that of earlier years. Formerly, adult children felt duty-bound to care for aging parents. Did not the Bible say, "Honor your father and your mother, so that your days may be long in the land that the LORD your God is giving you" (Exod. 20:12)?

So, fulfilling this commandment, adult children brought their older parents into their homes and cared for them.

This generation of older adults comes with a different perspective. We realize that our children carry heavy burdens, often sandwiched between our needs and their own. In many settings spouses work outside the home, making it impossible to provide full-time care to parents. Furthermore, many adult children still wrestle with the exhausting activities and demands of their own children. Those of us in later years now find it more acceptable to be cared for by other caregivers than by children whom we have reared and nurtured. My wife and I decided some years ago to determine our own future and not lay that on our children. When we told our children about our decision, they heaved a sigh of relief!

Yes, Paul did write, "Bear one another's burdens" (Gal. 6:2). But he added, "For all must carry their own loads" (Gal. 6:5). Paul seems to say, "Care for each other, but don't load your legitimate responsibilities on others." Adult children can carry burdens *with* aging parents, not *for* them. They can offer encouragement, help, and support; they may even suggest retirement options. But we are responsible for making decisions about our later years.

Dear Lord, we know the heavy responsibilities our children have. We are overwhelmed when we visit them and witness the flurry of activities and hectic schedules. Decisions are difficult; but in struggling with what to do in our later years and putting our plans into action, we make life easier for our children. Amen.

3 WHY THE DELAY?

Read Numbers 13:30–14:4

Caleb quieted the people before Moses, and said, "Let us go up at once and occupy it, for we are well able to overcome it." . . . So they [the ten spies] brought to the Israelites an unfavorable report of the land that they had spied out, saying, "The land . . . is a land that devours its inhabitants; and all the people . . . are of great size . . . ; and to ourselves we seemed like grasshoppers."

NUMBERS 13:30, 32-33

The Israelites emerge from forty years in the wilderness and camp at Kadesh. They stand on the brink of claiming God's promise of the land. Caleb and Joshua return from their mission with a positive report: with God's help the Israelites can defeat their enemies. But the majority report differs. The ten spies agree about the land's goodness, but they believe the enemies are too great to overcome. They fear the "giants" in the land who made them feel like grasshoppers.

"Grasshopperitis" is a common disease. Whenever we dwell on our fears and do not trust God's grace, we suffer from it. The Israelites side with the majority report and, because of lack of faith and delay, are denied the land.

Dr. Sam Stone, administrator of the Glenaire Retirement Community in Cary, North Carolina, talks about the transition from I'm Not Ready Yet to I Waited Too Long. Many people in later life, while still in reasonably good health, choose options other than a retirement community. They decide to stay in their homes or move to a resort location or refuse to think about their future. I can relate to that refusal!

At times I could scarcely fathom the notion that I would have to leave familiar surroundings to live in a place with a lot of old people and relinquish some of my cherished independence. Being in a retirement community seemed a scary proposition. The facility housed a number of frail people who faced ongoing diminishments. Being a chaplain to those people was one thing; living in their midst was quite another.

Yet I remembered many older people who waited too long to gain admittance to a retirement community and then faced placement in long-term care. I realized that delay might not be in my best self-interest. Why not act now, while still able, rather than wait until it was too late? Furthermore, my family had a history of strokes; if I experienced one, I did not want to be a burden to my wife.

The time had come to act. My wife and I faced our fears, checked our wallets, and visited several retirement communities. This was the *kairos* time, the right time for us to make this move before *chronos*, or clock time, ran out on us.

Like Caleb and Joshua, my wife and I spied out several retirement communities and found an affordable one near our daughter that seemed right for us. Many of our friends posed serious questions about our decision, and we often felt like Joshua and Caleb. But we believed that God had called us to this new beginning and would help us conquer our "grasshopperitis."

Keeper of our days, if only we can risk the unknown and not cling to the familiar, we will learn of your grace and strength. Amen.

4 DOWNSIZING

Read Luke 9:1-6

[Jesus] said to them [the disciples], "Take nothing for your journey."

LUKE 9:3

Jesus told the disciples to travel light; leave possessions behind. Don't let unnecessary baggage encumber you.

Once you decide that a move is desirable or necessary, the next step comes in downsizing. I heard of a man whose life decisions exemplified wise downsizing. In his fifties, he owned a big farm with many acres. When he reached his sixties he downsized to two acres. When he reached his seventies, he sold his farm and tilled a small garden. When he reached his eighties he gave up his garden and had a small flower box in his apartment window. He is now ninety-five and still enjoying his flowers.

Moving into an apartment with one-third our former space, my wife and I had to plan what we could keep—valuable furniture, cherished books, and other collections. The rest became history. We downsized our home, giving away or selling two-thirds of our furniture and possessions.

What decisions! What to give the children, what to donate to charities, what to sell in a yard sale? For me, my prized library was the hardest thing to downsize. But I selected the books I would keep and read again. My wife planned a small flower garden outside our apartment on the patio. We cleared out the clutter and simplified our lives.

In this life we ordinary folks will never achieve what Zen Buddhists call "stufflessness." But shedding things helps our soul grow. Jesus made it clear that "real life is not measured by how much we own" (Luke 12:15, NLT).

My wife and I tried to imagine living in a small apartment, stripped of the space and things that had blessed our lives. But we knew we would have to experience it before we could realize what it meant. Downsizing is a cleansing experience. Frank MacEowen has written,

> Eventually we get claustrophobic with all the clutter. . . . We grow tired of our possessions because they do not fill the void. They do not make us happy. They did not provide us with the sustained and sustainable *experience* of the inspirited life we were longing for in our bones.[3]

Self-emptying Christ, you lived such a simple life, devoid of wealth and possessions. Your soul was free, never distracted by things material. Help us to learn that as we simplify life, we come closer to you and realize you are our truest treasure. Amen.

5 WHAT OTHERS SAID

Read Ruth 1:1-18

> So [Naomi] set out from the place where she had been
> living, she and her two daughters-in-law, and they went
> on their way to go back to the land of Judah.
>
> RUTH 1:7

Picture the scene: three widows on their way to the land of Judah. Naomi, the oldest widow, is returning to her native land of Judah. Ruth and Orpah, younger widows and Ruth's daughters-in-law, forfeit their hopes for marriage by going to a strange land. Naomi persuades Orpah to return to Moab, but Ruth remains resolute in her commitment to Naomi.

We can imagine some of the comments of the Moabite women as they gather at the wells of marketplaces: "Why would Naomi leave Moab?" "The weather up north will be much colder." "Naomi has been gone so long that Judah will be a strange culture." They might have added, "Those folks speak a different language and worship a strange god." They shake their heads in disbelief at Ruth's decision to forsake her own people.

Naomi gives voice to her despair when she reaches Bethlehem. She says to the people of the town, "Don't call me Naomi. . . . Instead, call me Mara, for the Almighty has made life very bitter for me" (Ruth 1:20, NLT).

In many ways I can relate to this biblical story. I had spent most of my childhood and adolescent years in Pennsylvania; but after living fifty years in North Carolina, my wife and I decided to enter a retirement community in western

Pennsylvania near our daughter. It would be a great adventure to launch out in a new culture and make a new beginning. Our friends' responses to our decision to leave the community and go "up north" were many and varied One woman said, "I have suffered many losses recently and have considered doing the same thing." A younger woman stated wistfully, "I just wish my parents would make that decision. They think they can stay in their home forever."

A man in his fifties told us, "My mother won't even consider leaving her home, so I am trying to employ a full-time caregiver. But they are expensive and hard to find." Some of my older friends didn't want to listen to our plans. In denial about their own situation, they either ignored or envied our decision. I realized many of their responses did not indicate concern for us but for their own issues. As the Talmud states, "We don't see things as they are; we see things as we are."

Finally, a few supportive words emerged. My editor at Upper Room Books, JoAnn Miller, wrote, "You amaze me with your foresight and courage to take control of your life. Your experience may lead to something helpful to others as they face a similar circumstance."

A friend commented, "Your move has made me think. I will consider options and talk with my children. If my children have to make the decision for my wife and me, at least they won't be in the dark about our preferences."

Naomi was returning to her home, which no doubt had changed considerably since her departure. But, like Ruth, my wife and I began the journey into the unknown.

Lord, make me aware that what matters in my choices is not others' opinions but following your guidance. Amen.

6 MOVING ON, NOT LOOKING BACK

Read Luke 9:51-62

Jesus said to him, "No one who puts a hand to the plow and looks back is fit for the kingdom of God."

LUKE 9:57

An enthusiastic man decides to follow Jesus, but first he wants to party and say good-bye to people at home. One last blast before hitting the road! Jesus tells him to forget those plans at home and to hit the road of discipleship.

We wonder why Jesus makes such a strong demand on this man. What's wrong with farewell parties and good-byes? Jesus knows that a plowman who does not keep his eye constantly on the goal toward which he moves cannot plow a straight furrow. Jesus knows that a lingering visit to old loyalties might weaken this man's commitment to the kingdom. To follow Jesus means a radical break with the old lifestyle.

Jesus' words resounded in my heart as my wife and I made our final plans to leave our home and move into a new retirement community. We had stayed long in that town. When former Alabama basketball coach Wimp Sanderson retired after thirty-two years as coach, he commented, "I've been here so long that when I came the Dead Sea wasn't even sick!"

While we had accomplished much in our community, the time had come to move on. The signs of God's hand in this decision seemed so apparent. We found an affordable apartment in a new retirement community near our daughter and her family. We sold our house in two days, which had never happened in earlier transactions. The time had come to put our hand to the plow and not look back.

Despite some sleepless nights wrestling with God over this decision, my wife and I finally came to a sense of peace about it. Our outward circumstances and an inner voice convinced us that God was calling us to this life. We found it difficult to stay in our North Carolina community once everyone learned we were leaving. We had so many farewells to say to so many people we loved. Anyone who has experienced these good-byes knows how hard they are. You stand in receiving lines and hardly know what to say. Your friends say nice things, but their words make you sad.

The in-between time is always a tough period. Interims seem to take an eternity of time. Some people even questioned our move and encouraged us to change our minds. One friend suggested that after a while we would be back. Another offered help in acquiring a condo in the town's retirement community. It was a gut-wrenching time.

A former mentor and professor, Dr. Donald Miller, was called to the presidency of Pittsburgh Theological Seminary. He responded, "I am not going to Pittsburgh, even if it is the will of God!" But he went, and God blessed his ministry.

So I appreciate Jesus' challenge. We had made our decision. Our hearts and hands remained focused on the move. There was no going back now!

God of our lives, you have been our help in all the journeys we have made. Now we believe the time is right to leave the familiar and launch out into the unknown. Be our guide and stay. Amen.

REFLECTIVE EXERCISES

- A couple says, "We are in reasonably good health and are managing our home quite well. I know we are getting older, but what's the hurry about making changes?" Do you agree with them? If not, why not?

- You have decided to enter a Continuing Care Retirement Community (CCRC). List the questions you would ask the director of marketing when you visit.

- A couple with modest income say they cannot even consider a CCRC because "those places are for a wealthy clientele." Is that true? How do you find out?

- Fantasize the "perfect" retirement community for you. Write down your fantasy on paper.

- Make two lists. First, valued possessions you would want to take with you to a CCRC. Second, other items you would give to your children, sell at a yard sale, or give to charities.

- Think of times in your journey when you faced a life change that seemed too big for you but which you felt called to pursue. What distracted or blocked you from making this change? What happened? In what ways might your handling of that event affect your later life decisions?

THE JOURNEY BEGINS

The First Weeks

So there is always in life a place to leave
and a new place to find, and in between
a zone of hesitation and uncertainty
tinged with more or less intense anxiety.[4]

—PAUL TOURNIER

7 LIKE ABRAM AND SARAI

Read Genesis 12:1-4

> The LORD had said to Abram, "Leave your country, your people and your father's household and go to the land I will show you". . . . So Abram left, as the LORD had told him. . . . He took his wife Sarai.
>
> GENESIS 12:1, 4-5 (NIV)

"So Abram left." These three words from the book of Genesis reveal so much pain and commitment. At age seventy-five, Abram and Sarai leave all that is familiar—their country and their people—to become God's pilgrims. They leave a land already highly populated and highly developed for that time. They have no organized tour or MapQuest to follow, not even a sure destination. They make the long, treacherous trek across the desert sands to a new country. All this because of a call from God.

My wife and I could identify with Abram and Sarai. I have always believed that Abram took the initiative, and Sarai went along somewhat reluctantly. Like Sarai, my wife must have wondered if this old man really knew what he was doing, and at our age! Like Sarai, she loved her home and her friends. Like Sarai, she went along with her husband, although at times she did think I was out of my mind.

I can almost hear the shocked reaction of the people of Ur. What is wrong with Abram? Who is this strange God that he hears calling him to this insane venture across the desert? Many of our friends also questioned our decision to leave a community where we both had invested so much, to enter a retirement community five hundred miles away.

Unlike us, some people choose to enter retirement communities near their homes. It makes sense. Although downsizing to an apartment brings its challenges, at least they remain in familiar territory and can maintain relationships with friends. They have no new territory to confront but can still walk the streets of their community, shop in the same stores, attend their church.

For us, however, the journey required that we leave a lifetime of work and joy in a chosen community to venture across the miles to a new life. We knew it would be demanding and hard, but my wife and I both felt God's call in this venture. We thought of the words of the apostle Paul to the Philippians, "I am confident of this, that the one who began a good work among you will bring it to completion" (Phil. 1:6).

On a warm spring day, the moving van arrived. We said our good-byes to some friends, and the journey began. It felt strange to drive past the town where we had planned to remain forever and to set out on the road to a new life.

God of new beginnings, you call us in strange ways, often disrupting our customary life to make pilgrimages of faith. When we hear that call and obey, sustain and strengthen us for what lies ahead. Amen.

8 DISORIENTED AT FIRST

Read Philippians 4

"I have no peace, no quietness. I have no rest; instead,
only trouble comes."

JOB 3:26 (NLT)

My wife and I arrived at our destination on a warm, beautiful afternoon. Our moving van arrived without incident and the movers brought our furniture into the apartment. It was a memorable day, as we lined up fifty boxes of belongings we could not squeeze into our apartment. We wondered if we would ever be free of the chaos.

After major transitions of life, it is wise not to make quick decisions, as the shock of change leaves you disoriented. However, moving into a retirement community compels you to make quick decisions. Where to place the furniture? Where will the cat live? When do we change addresses on our driver's licenses and insurance policies?

The first few days run together. The day we moved in, some residents came to greet us. Later we couldn't find Cinderella, our cat. I panicked and imagined that in all the confusion she had escaped from the apartment and wandered down the strange halls. Imagine our relief when we found her huddled in one of our suitcases!

One redeeming aspect of retirement apartments is the storage unit for items that do not fit into the apartment. After hauling some our belongings to the storage unit, I was so disoriented that I put the lock on upside down. I had to track down the maintenance man to cut it off.

I made a major blunder on our first visit to local restaurant. I wore my Philadelphia Eagles hat and wondered why I got so many hard stares. Finally, a man kindly said, "Up here, we are Steelers fans."

Repeatedly, while trying to make calls on the new phone, I dialed my own number. Trying to learn so many new names overwhelmed me. I felt brain dead. The resident directory was out of date and not much help. I called Gert, Mert and Mrs. Bowers, Mrs. Bowser. All the older women looked alike; I wondered if I could ever learn their names. The young campus manager visited us and gave three pieces of advice. (1) Take your time. Pace yourself. You can't do it all at once. (2) Try to reach out to residents and learn their names. (3) Visit assisted living. (At that time I wondered why; later, I knew.) Perhaps some of my disorientation was due to my compulsive need to get everything done right away.

As my wife and I strolled around our building at twilight, I thought of the words of John Greenleaf Whittier,

> Drop thy still dews of quietness,
> till all our striving cease;
> take from our souls the strain and stress,
> and let our ordered lives confess
> the beauty of thy peace.[5]

At that moment, amid the chaos and confusion, I doubted that our lives would ever have any order or that we would ever feel at home here.

God of peace, help us not to feel bad about being disoriented but to realize this too will pass, and we will find peace. Amen.

9 MUSIC AT MIDNIGHT

Read Acts 16:23-34

About midnight Paul and Silas were praying and singing
hymns to God, and the prisoners were listening to them.

ACTS 16:25

One of my favorite stories in the Bible comes from a Philippian jail at midnight. Paul and Silas are imprisoned in this
dark, dank cell, their feet fastened in stocks. But they sing
hymns, and even the prisoners listen to them. I always wondered what they sang. Was it songs of Zion or new hymns
celebrating the Christian faith?

One evening my wife and I made our weary way upstairs,
pushing a cart of boxes to the storage unit. It had been
another long, tiring day of unpacking, sorting, and decid-
ing what could fit in our apartment.

As we left the storage unit, suddenly, like magic, we heard
someone playing beautiful music on a piano. It was like
manna from heaven. We stopped in the hallway and listened
for a while. Later a resident told me the pianist was Mark
Markosky, a resident in assisted living. Mark was a musician
who had sung with the Pittsburgh Opera Company and the
Don Cossack Chorus, which had toured throughout the
United States and Europe. When his family brought him to
the retirement community, Mark insisted on bringing his
piano; and often he blessed residents with his impromptu
concerts. His gift of music lifted our souls that late night. In
a way we could identify with the prisoners in the Philippian
jail, for we still felt confined by our small space.

Once there were two organists in a cathedral town. On Sundays they took turns playing for High Mass. Both knew their music and played so well the old organ seemed to speak. Yet the two musicians played differently. People who knew little about music felt the difference. Most were drawn to the older organist and did not know why.

One Sunday, after an especially dazzling performance by the older organist, the younger spoke to him following the concert. "I heard you play today. I could have played every note you did, but somehow my music would not sound like yours. Your whole soul seemed to escape into the melody."

The older man smiled an embarrassed smile and replied, "You are right. My soul is in my music and so is yours and so is the soul of every person in the church who tries to sing. As you grow older and suffer more, your soul will grow also. As it does, it will fill with a unique beauty all its own."

Like that older organist, Mark had suffered some of the losses of later life. His memory was failing; he often wandered and got confused. But he could still play that piano with soul. His music lifted our spirits that night, which seemed like midnight.

Thank you, blessed Lord, for sending us songs in the midnight of our lives. When we feel discouraged and tired, we rest beside the road and hear the angels sing. Amen.

10 WELCOMED BY FAMILY

Read Psalm 68

God sets the lonely in families.

PSALM 68:6 (NIV)

Our first few days and weeks here were a blur of new faces and strange places. It was almost like getting the wrong pair of glasses from an optician. (That happened to me once, and I thought I was going blind!) We knew no one and felt like strangers in a foreign land. Moving to a new location is always a challenge, but we were in a new culture and a far-off state from our home. We had moved from the south to the north, where *y'alls* were replaced by *yinz*!

Repeatedly someone would ask, "Why in the world would you come north to retire? Most northerners migrate to the South to retire." This felt like a rerun of what we heard before we left the South. "Why go up there when the weather is so bitter cold in the winter and face all that snow and zero weather?" Well, at least I didn't have to shovel the snow!

Our decision to move north to retire hinged on two simple facts: (1) an affordable retirement community for folks of modest means and (2) our daughter, Anna Katherine, and her family lived ten minutes from our new residence. Anna and her husband, David Sever, helped smooth the rough places, offering help and support. They opened their home to us, showed us how to navigate the area, invited us for meals, and did many random acts of kindness for us.

Our two granddaughters, Brannon and ReidAnn, were instant joys. They even hung a sign in our apartment that greeted us upon our arrival, *Welcome Gammie and Gramps!* They cheered our spirits with their innate curiosity, clever sayings, and love of life. Soon they were bounding around our retirement community, charming all the residents.

I empathize with residents who have no living family or whose family lives at a distance from them. Although many of them formerly lived in this community, they feel isolated without family nearby. One new resident told me, "It is so hard to adjust here. I lived over fifty years in the same house, and I have no family." I suggested she come to our Coffee Klatch at 10:00 AM twice a week. She responded, "Sorry. I never get up that early." Maybe we should start a Coffee Klatch at night too!

We are blessed by our relationship with the Sever family. I believe that as the days unfold, we will be getting involved in the girls' activities and watching them grow and mature.

It will take time to feel accepted in this retirement community. So many of the residents are what I call the "Mayflower people" because they were here when the facility opened. We are newcomers and often feel that our opinions and views are not heard. Patience brings acceptance.

However, we can become "family" here too. We need to get out of the apartment, mingle with residents, and find new friends. I have always believed that older people prefer a few close friends, rather than large crowds. That is certainly true in a retirement community.

At the beginning of Creation, the first time God said, "Not good," was when God said, "It is not good for the man to be alone" (Gen. 2:18, NIV). As the psalmist said, "God sets the lonely in families." We are blessed with having a family nearby.

But we will also be ambassadors of hospitality to those who have no family nearby, as we seek to find a family here.

We give thanks, O gracious Parent, for all who have shown hospitality to us in our lives and made us feel we are part of their family. Amen.

11 WALK AND NOT FAINT

Read Isaiah 40:27-31

> Those who hope in the LORD
>   will renew their strength.
> They will soar on wings like eagles;
>   they will run and not grow weary,
>   they will walk and not be faint.
>
> ISAIAH 40:31 (NIV)

One of the first things I noticed at this retirement community was the walkway around the building. My wife and I would often walk outside, drinking in the wonder of God's world. At times we saw young fawns grazing on the hillside or woodchucks pausing from their dinner to look at us. The sunsets were spectacular, and we looked forward to stepping outside our apartment and entering another world.

Often we would meet other residents on the walks. Some would inch along on their walkers, determined to make their rounds. Others would rest on the benches, deep in thought. We saw couples, married over sixty years, sitting on the benches, holding hands. It reminded me of a picture that depicts a couple sitting on a bench with these words by Robert Sexton (see www.robertsexton.com)as the caption:

> When we grow old
> I will find two chairs
> and set them close
> each sun-lit day,
> that you and I—in quiet joy—may rock
> the world away.

One early morning I stopped and talked with an older man who told me his story. He said, "I am not a religious man, but every morning I say, 'God, I am here. What do you want me to do?'" His comment seemed more religious to me than pious performances and meaningless rituals.

Many evenings volunteers from independent living would shepherd residents with Alzheimer's disease around the building. It was the highlight of the residents' day to be outside, soaking in the beauty of nature. Walking releases endorphins and reduces stress. When older people are able, walking provides the best exercise. I discovered in those early days of adjustment that walking helped me walk through problems and sort my thoughts out. Walking also provided time to talk with God.

The prophet of the exile boosts the people's spirits with God's promise of a new beginning. He reminds them that this God possesses the power to raise up the fainthearted and the exhausted. Those who place their hope and confidence in this God may "run and not grow weary, they will walk and not faint." Those moments of quiet reflection as I walked around the building gave me hope and confidence that God would provide the strength to see my wife and me through this new chapter in our lives.

Two people walked that dusty road from Jerusalem to Emmaus on that first Easter afternoon. A stranger joined them and conversed with them as they walked. Only later did they realize it was Jesus himself who walked with them. It may well be that this living Christ walked with me and strengthened my heart.

Living Christ, you walked the roads of Galilee with your disciples when you came to this world. Your presence transformed every road they took, every walk they made. Whenever we step outside our homes to walk in the Father's world, visit us with your presence. Amen.

12 THOSE EXCITING FIRST WEEKS

Read Psalm 126

When the LORD restored his exiles to Jerusalem,
　it was like a dream!

. . . .

Yes, the LORD has done amazing things for us!
　What joy!

PSALM 126:1, 3 (NLT)

It's hard to imagine the jubilation of those exiles when they return to Jerusalem after seventy years in Babylon. They rejoice as once again they walk the streets of the city and plant their feet on holy ground. How excited and exuberant they must have felt at first. The long, hard years in Babylon are forgotten in their excitement and joy to be home.

The first weeks in our new retirement community were like a dream. We fixed up our apartment, giving everything its proper place. I rejoiced when shelves arrived to give the remnant of my library a new home.

We spent most of the summer becoming acquainted with our new area. We visited historic sites and learned about the French and Indian Wars in western Pennsylvania. We took trips to Pittsburgh, visited museums, attended concerts on the lawn, and saw the sights of a large metropolitan city. With other residents we took a boat ride down the river and saw where three rivers converged. As an avid baseball fan, I had to pinch myself to see if I was dreaming as I sat at PNC Park and watched major league baseball.

We took our granddaughters on trips to reenactments of battles and an eighteenth-century inn where travelers stopped to rest. It was so new and exciting. North Carolina seemed centuries away.

My wife and I reached out to residents, trying to make friends. At mealtimes we intentionally sat with different residents. In that way we learned about the history of the area, as well as their life stories. We were experiencing euphoria as we made new friends and explored this area. In fact, one of our sons in California wrote another son and asked, "Has anyone seen our parents?" We were gone that much.

One night we attended a concert by the Pittsburgh Symphony. I sat in a lobby, waiting for my wife, and suddenly realized that many people walked by me, and no one knew me! The anonymity overwhelmed me. While sad to be such a stranger, I felt relieved to be by myself with no pressures.

In my former community, I could not walk down the streets of the village without someone stopping to talk or make some request for more of my "volunteer" time. Often I felt squeezed by the pressure and stress of trying to do too much, like an overpacked suitcase ready to burst.

Here my experience differed. No one put any pressure on me, so I could make my own way and find my place at my own pace.

We visited several churches until finally we found a church home that resonated with who we were. We could worship God, enjoy the people, and be free from the church politics that had often plagued our days.

The first few weeks were indeed exciting and new. But it was the calm before the storm. Soon the newness would wear off, and I would find myself wondering, *What have I done? Why did I ever leave and come here?*

God of surprises, when we face new beginnings, help us to realize that they may be marvelous and great, not something to dread. Amen.

13 SACRAMENTAL MEALS

Read Acts 2:37-47

> Day by day, as they spent much time together in the temple, they broke bread at home and ate their food with glad and generous hearts, praising God and having the goodwill of all the people.
>
> ACTS 2:46-47

You cannot scan the Bible from cover to cover without recognizing the importance of meals. The Hebrews celebrated the Passover meal to commemorate their deliverance from Egypt. Jesus ate the Passover meal with the disciples and instituted the Lord's Supper. Often throughout Jesus' ministry, mealtime was a sacramental experience. Martha of Bethany often prepared meals for Jesus, and he told many stories about meals and banquets.

Luke describes the life of the early church in the second volume of his history (Acts) and includes meals as times for fellowship and unity. They partook of food "with glad and generous hearts" is Luke's description of mealtime in the early church.

Meals have special meaning in a retirement community. Food and company are pleasures older people can still enjoy. It is a time to relax and enjoy conversation with other residents. We often enjoyed talking about current events and learning about Pennsylvania during the meals. Many of our table talks turned into listening to life stories or sharing issues in our community. It is the peak time to socialize and to see people you rarely see otherwise. It amused me to see how two of our ninety-year-old resident men dressed up every evening as if they were going out to dinner.

During the first weeks when my wife and I went to eat in the dining room, we decided not to sit at the same place or eat with the same people every night. However, we noted that some residents did prefer to sit at the same table each evening, often with the same friends. We also began to realize that when residents invited us to eat with them, it was a symbol of acceptance.

Unexpected things happen in the dining room. One woman had a massive coronary and died. One night we noticed a new resident eating by himself and, knowing how it felt to be "the new kids on the block," we went over and sat with him. Suddenly he burst into tears. He had planned to enter this community with his wife who, several weeks before their arrival, had died. He had to make the difficult transition by himself. He seemed so vulnerable and sad, still locked in his grief. Our hearts went out to him. Later he became one of my best friends.

In any retirement community mealtime is crucial. The director of dining services gets more comments and criticisms than any other staff member. "The steak was too cold." "The napkins weren't properly folded." "The silverware was dirty," and "Why did you take our white tablecloths from us?" I always expressed gratitude to the kitchen staff and the young servers whose presence brightened our days.

I thought to myself: *Most all of us came from homes where families gathered at mealtime to talk about their day.* Unlike some modern homes, where family members rush through meals to go to soccer or other events and eat in front of the

TV, mealtime for our generation was a special moment. Like those early Christians who celebrated their common life in Christ, our mealtimes here become sacramental.

Lord Jesus, you enjoyed eating with all kinds of people and never excluded anyone from your table. As we eat together today, grant that we may reach across barriers and build bridges. Amen.

14 MY PRAYER COMES HOME

Read Psalm 34

I sought the LORD, and he answered me,
    and delivered me from all my fears.

· ·

This poor soul cried, and was heard by the LORD,
    and was saved from every trouble.

PSALM 34:4, 6

Several weeks before we moved, I was an honored guest at the library where I had volunteered for several years. One of the librarians read a prayer that sounded vaguely familiar. Midway through the prayer, it dawned on me that it was a prayer I had written and published three years before! I wrote this prayer for people entering a retirement community.

Well, Lord, the day has come. In many ways I dreaded leaving my home, my security. And now I have to give up some of my privacy and live with other old people. Help me even now to accept these people as I find them—boring at times, stimulating and garrulous. Help me remember that all these people are loved by you. Deliver me from being snappy at meals with people who are cranky—they may be in pain. If someone wants to confide a problem, help me listen. And may I reach out to those when I feel the urge to strike out. As I leave my home, give me a sense of call, even as you called old Abraham and Sarah as they left their home on a new journey of faith. If I can love my neighbor there, then I have a mission. Amen.[6]

How wrong I was in one aspect of my prayer. During these first weeks I have learned to appreciate and respect these residents. My experience did not support my prayer's perceptions. These are courageous, hardy folk here. Most have worked hard all their lives and deserve their retirement. I have found no elitism or snobbery here. So I revised my prayer in light of my experience in this community:

Lord, despite my struggle to surrender my past and cling to the familiar, I am now moving on into new beginnings. Forgive me, Lord, for my misconceptions of what this place would be and my foolish fears about my life here.

My first weeks here have been happy times, and no one could have been more warmly welcomed than we were. I give you thanks for all the people I meet here every day in the mail room, in the halls, in the dining room. They are real people, with no pretense or inordinate preoccupation with themselves. Their courage and winter grace, despite so many diminishments, inspire me. I appreciate the way they have gently welcomed us into their community and made us feel at home. I treasure moments when they have opened their hearts and told me their stories. I value their privacy, and they respect mine. Lord, you have called me to this place, where every day is an opportunity for ministry. Amen.

Teach me, O God, to be silent in your presence before I frame words that I may one day regret. Teach me as I listen to you. May the words of my mouth and the meditation of my heart be what you intend, not what I am thinking. Amen.

REFLECTIVE EXERCISES

- Imagine this is your first day in a retirement community. You have sold your house, downsized your possessions, and arrived at your new "home." What does that feel like? What will you expect in this new lifestyle?

- Someone has said, "The greatest risk is to take no risks." What risks have you taken in your life? How does your willingness to take risks relate to entering a retirement community?

- Sometimes first impressions can be misleading. How might this be true in a move to a retirement community?

- When in your life have transitions or changes disoriented you? How did you act? What did you do?

- Recall mealtimes in your family of origin and your present family. What meaning did they have for you? for those around the table? How might this meaning carry over to mealtimes in a retirement community?

- A friend has just left her home where she had lived for many years and gone to a retirement community miles from her former home. Write a prayer for her.

SECOND THOUGHTS

Months One and Two

∾

The great interruptions of life leave us completely disoriented. The map of life changes overnight and our sense of direction and purpose goes with it. Life comes to a halt, takes on a new and indiscernible shape. . . . What was is no more and what is to come, if anything, is unclear.

—Joan D. Chittister

15 HAVING SECOND THOUGHTS

Read Exodus 14:5-8; 16:1-3

> When the king of Egypt was told that the people had fled, the minds of Pharaoh and his officials were changed toward the people, and they said, "What have we done, letting Israel leave our service?"
>
> ... The whole congregation of the Israelites complained against Moses and Aaron in the wilderness. The Israelites said to them, "If only we had died by the hand of the LORD in the land of Egypt."
>
> EXODUS 14:5; 16:2-3

Although they are deadly enemies, the pharaoh of Egypt and the Israelites have something in common: second thoughts about their decisions. Pharaoh realizes he has made a mistake by allowing all that slave labor to leave Egypt. So he sends his border police to stop their escape.

Even though they have seen the wonder of Yahweh's plunging the horse and rider into the sea and miraculously delivering them from the Egyptians, the Israelites have second thoughts about leaving Egypt. They want to return to an existence they know rather than face the unknown wilderness. Later they will express the same feelings even when God provides food in the desert for them.

I admit I began to have second thoughts about leaving the town I loved and where I had planned to end my days. I had envisioned my final days in a room surrounded by my library. I had even purchased niches in a columbarium at the church for our cremains. The initial euphoria had worn off, and I felt suspended in a limbo between a life I loved and a life yet to come.

I began tormenting myself with such questions as, *What have I done? Was it really the best time? Why didn't we wait a few more years until our funds would allow us to live in a retirement community nearer our home? Why was I so impulsive?*

I had experienced some real regrets about leaving the community that helped define my existence. The new place was not all that I thought it would be. People kept asking us, "What are you doing here? You look so young." "Here, we see North Carolina as the perfect place to retire. Why would you leave there to come here?"

As I struggled with these second thoughts, I took a long walk, talked to myself and with God. I knew God would not reject my honest doubts. Along the walk, I felt God gave me some other questions. *What if the Israelites had turned back to Egypt and abandoned Moses?* That would have made the Exodus a farce and their future a broken dream. *What if we had gone back and tried to make a new beginning in our old community?* It would never be the same; you can't go back without being disillusioned by the changes. You just don't go home again!

It took the discipline of the desert to forge a new beginning for the Hebrews. When life became hard, the temptation would return. But God strengthened them for the journey. Later when the cold winter caused unexpected illness for me, I again had second thoughts. I idealized my former life in the warm South. But God would give me strength to stand by my convictions. Second thoughts are a normal part of tough decisions. Constant faith that God is in this new life will see us through.

Ever-present God, in our struggles, grant us courage and resolve. We do not ask to see the distant scene but need the assurance of the present moment. Yesterday is history; the future is mystery; and today is a gift—the present! Amen.

16 PLAY THE BALL WHERE THE MONKEY DROPS IT

Read Jeremiah 29:1-9

Seek the welfare of the city where I have sent you into exile, and pray to the LORD on its behalf, for in its welfare you will find your welfare.

JEREMIAH 29:7

A story is told in Calcutta, India, of a golf course where monkeys would drop out of the trees, pick up the golf balls, and scurry across the golf course. As they ran, they would drop the golf balls here and there. Despite efforts to control the monkeys by building fences and trapping them, nothing worked. The golfers adopted an unusual rule: Play the ball where the monkey drops it.

You can imagine how those monkeys wreaked havoc with the golfers' games. A beautiful drive down the center of the fairway might be picked up by one of those monkeys and dropped in the rough. On the other hand, a slice or a hook might be flung onto the fairway. The golfers soon realized that golf on that course was similar to life: there are good breaks and bad breaks.

Jeremiah writes a letter to the exiles in Babylon who may have expected deliverance, like the Exodus from Egypt. Instead, Jeremiah tells them to settle down in this foreign land and work for the welfare of the city. "Play the ball where the monkey drops it." No use pining for Jerusalem. No sense in dreaming about a glorious return. Settle down and work for the welfare of Babylon.

I began to realize it is a waste of effort to torture myself with regrets and remorse. Although some of the joyful moments of my former community kept returning, I knew I needed to work for the welfare of this community. However, I felt it would be a long time before I could really settle down.

I began by talking with the program director and volunteering to help residents in assisted living and dementia care. I also helped initiate a religious life committee that designed some new approaches to worship and pastoral care for residents in the apartments. I believed that "in [the community's] welfare you will find your welfare."

Anyone living in a retirement community soon realizes that this is life's stopping place. This awesome realization generates some remorse over leaving a community where you did not experience this understanding. Many of our new friends would become extremely frail; others would die. It seemed that the emergency medical service ambulance appeared every day to take someone to the hospital. But this is the reality of being here. My wife and I made the choice. The monkey had dropped the ball here. So we need to play the game of life from this vantage point.

I began to realize that transitions of life do leave us disoriented. The course of our life changes overnight, and life has come to a halt. "What used to be is no more; what is to come, if anything, is unclear." That was the reality I now faced as I yearned for my old home.

As time passed, Jeremiah's word became all the more a reality. The exiles realized that their hoped-for deliverance was not on the horizon then—perhaps not in their lifetimes. So they settled in to make the most of living in a strange culture.

One of our new neighbors said to us, "We're glad you are here. You can make a difference to all of us." But I wasn't really sure. One morning I asked a resident, "How are you feeling?" He replied, "It's too early to tell." I felt the same way.

Lord of change, help us to be content where we are. May we see others as Christ sees them as we work for their welfare. Amen.

17 FEELING TRAPPED

Read Exodus 14:9-13, 21-23

The Egyptians . . . pursued the Israelites and overtook
them as they camped by the sea. . . .

   As Pharaoh approached, the Israelites looked up, and
there were the Egyptians, marching after them. They were
terrified.

Exodus 14:9-10 (NIV)

At one time or another everyone can identify with the terrified Israelites as they seem trapped at the Sea of Reeds.
Pharaoh's border police are rushing toward them with their
weapons of mass destruction, and before them looms the
sea. But Yahweh makes a way through the sea to safety on
the other shore. The Israelites believe themselves trapped,
facing sure disaster. In reality, they are on their way to a new
destiny.

At times residents in a retirement community may feel
trapped, especially in the early weeks and months. One new
resident, who had lived in a spacious home on a lake front,
told me, "I felt I had moved into a motel, and it was time to
check out and go home." Another said, "I'm glad I can still
drive. There are moments when the walls of my apartment
close in on me, and I just have to get out of this 'institution.'"
Imagine the feelings of residents who cannot drive and have
to depend on other people or the community van to get out
of the building.

During my first weeks and months there were moments
when I felt trapped. I longed for the former days when I

moved around our spacious home or wandered the streets of the town where we lived. Little did I know that the bitter Pennsylvania winter would really close me in as I battled respiratory disease and had to stay within the apartment and the community.

I came to my senses. I experienced no miraculous deliverance, as did the Israelites. But I realized that my life was here and now. I felt somewhat ashamed of my complaints, since many older people could not afford a community like this. I hummed the words of the hymn by Sarah Williams,

> Because I knew not when my life was good,
> And when there was a light upon my path,
> But turned my soul perversely to the dark,
>   O Lord, I do repent.

I realized how blessed I am and felt that every experience in my spiritual journey led to another level of growth. It is not so much what happens to us in life as how we respond. Even our desolations can become consolations! I have never had an easy life. It seemed at every twist and turn of my spiritual journey difficulties threatened to hem me in and stifle my growth.

Sometimes God places us in new situations for our own spiritual growth. Only through these challenges can God shape and transform our lives.

> *God of our deliverance, you save us from ourselves and our selfish preoccupations. When we feel trapped, it may well be the dawn of a better day. Give us faith to believe that "the best is yet to be." Amen.*

18 THE NOONDAY DEMON

Read Psalm 42

Do not be afraid of the terrors of the night,
　　nor fear the dangers of the day,
nor dread the plague that stalks in darkness,
　　nor the disaster that strikes at midday.

PSALM 91:5-6 (NLT)

The ancient monks would recite the Psalms daily. When they recited Psalm 91, they referred to the "disaster that strikes at midday" as the "noonday demon." This demon was their constant struggle with depression. Over 25 percent of older people are diagnosed with depression; often it is undiagnosed and untreated. People in a retirement community are especially vulnerable to depression. Confinement to a smaller space, loss of home, and the endless monotony of retirement living can cause depression. It can become a nightmare in slow motion. Some prefer to sleep rather than be active, and others isolate themselves in their room.

Many great souls battled the noonday demon all their lives: Abraham Lincoln, Ludwig von Beethoven, Winston Churchill, and William James. Persons who suffer from depression are in noble company!

During the early weeks and months at the retirement community, I admit I suffered from depression. The simplest acts demanded herculean effort. I felt like a package, wrapped up in myself, and began ruminating instead of living. I spent a fair amount of time reminiscing over what I had lost instead of living what I had gained.

The author of Psalm 42 knew depression. He cries out, "My heart is breaking as I remember how it used to be . . . Why am I discouraged? Why so sad?" (Psalm 42:4-5, NLT). I identified with his sadness as he remembers what he has lost. He recalls the thundering cataracts that pour down in springtime from the snows of Mount Hermon. Exiled, he is homesick for God's house.

Shallow words and pious platitudes do not help those who suffer from depression. Some offer glib answers without realizing the depths into which people sink when they are depressed. Like the psalmist, those in depression seek answers in the depths not the shallows.

The psalmist cries, "Deep calls to deep. . . . Hope in God" (42:7, 11). We need to embrace the mystery. The deeper we go into the heart's darkness to confront this noonday demon, the closer we get to the ultimate mystery of God.

I found no answers. Medication helped. I realized I had to work through this depression the best I could. My only answer came in realizing the depths of the Mystery. God stood with me as I battled the noonday demon. There would be light at the end of the tunnel, a way out of the darkness. As the psalmist finally exclaims, "I will put my hope in God! I will praise him again—my Savior and my God" (42:11, NLT). My faith kept me going in those dark moments when depression almost engulfed me.

God of hope, we bring our wounded hearts and broken spirits to you. You never reject those who struggle with doubt and depression. Calm our hearts and give us hope. Amen.

19 CONFRONTING ANXIETY

Read Matthew 6:25-33

"Therefore I tell you, do not worry about your life . . .
Can any of you by worrying add a single hour to your
span of life?"

MATTHEW 6:25, 27

If there is any validity to the gene bank, I must have inherited a major deposit of anxiety genes from my mother. She worried constantly, and so do I. We both would worry when we had nothing to worry about! But we are not alone. Surveys of primary physicians report that one-third of office visits are prompted by some form of anxiety. Those of us who live in retirement communities worry about health problems. When the ambulance arrives at the front door to take a resident to the hospital, we worry that one day it will come for us. When our neighbors become sick, we get anxious about when we may face that disease.

We worry about stretching our finances to meet the rising cost of living and increase in apartment rent. As our friends leave for assisted living or skilled care, we wonder how we will afford that setting when our time comes. We worry about the welfare of our families and experience anxiety on behalf of our grandchildren as we consider the world that awaits them.

Jesus asked, "Can any of you by worrying add a single hour to your span of life?" Anxiety is an exercise in futility. Like sitting in a rocking chair, it gives us something to do but gets us nowhere. One of the root meanings of the word *anxiety* is "strangle." We know the feeling when we get anxious. It strangles our activity and paralyzes our thoughts.

Medication can take the edge off, but that is not the final answer. My years as a chaplain in a nursing home convinced me that too many residents were overmedicated instead of given personal care that involved talking with them, validating their feelings, and allowing them to vent their anxieties.

During my anxious life, as I have battled this disease, I found ways to deal with my anxiety. I began to relate these methods to the anxiety of living in a retirement community.

1. Don't catastrophize. Refuse to let simple concerns become major anxieties.

2. Practice positive imaging. Chronic worriers tend to be preoccupied with fearful, negative thoughts.

3. Reach out to others. Look around and find someone in need, and help her or him.

4. Rely on God through constant prayer.

As I struggled with second thoughts about leaving the past and moving here, I realized much of my anxiety centered on that struggle. When initial plans and strategies for this new life failed, I refused to say, "Ain't it awful" and tried not to let that get me down. I tried to lighten up and laugh at my foibles and faux pas. When I got out of myself and listened to others, I found peace.

Jesus was the great physician. He gave us a solid prescription for anxiety: When we have done all we can to conquer our fears, the bottom line remains, "Trust a loving God."

O Christ, who battled that agonizing anxiety in the garden, we know you understand and care for us in all our anxieties. Amen.

20 SOMEONE SLIPPED AND FELL

Read 1 Samuel 4:11-22

The messenger rushed over to Eli, who was ninety-eight years old and blind. . . .

When the messenger mentioned what had happened to the Ark, Eli fell backward from his seat beside the gate.

1 SAMUEL 4:14-15, 18 (NLT)

At the weekly sing-along, some of the lyrics struck an uncomfortable chord with older people. The words raise the issue of someone's having fallen and goes on to inquire if you are that person. I began thinking about how many people here had fallen, injuring hips, backs, and wrists. A fall often means trips to the hospital and long months of rehabilitation. "Someone slipped and fell . . ." But I never dreamed it would be me!

I had fallen before, often because I did not watch my step. Once I slipped on a wet floor in a nursing home. An aide, not realizing I was the chaplain, said, "Well, Pop (terrible ageist term), if you're not careful we'll put you in a wheelchair!"

This fall was different. I had disciplined myself to walk on the treadmill every day. My usual speed is two-and-one-half to three miles per hour. I was sailing along, burning up the treadmill, when I realized I needed to slow down. Regrettably I pushed the forward button, and my speed raced to five miles per hour. I fell off the treadmill and onto the floor, only suffering some sore ribs. I am glad no one witnessed that embarrassment.

Eli, ninety-eight years old, had a much more serious fall, and it killed him! The messenger returns with the bad news that the Israelites, having suffered a great slaughter of their troops, have fled from the Philistines. He goes on to report that Eli's sons have been killed—a hard blow for old Eli. But when Eli learns that the sacred ark that houses the very presence of God has fallen into Philistine hands, he falls off his seat beside the gate, breaks his neck, and dies.

When Saul of Tarsus had the vision of the living Christ on the road to Damascus, he fell to the ground and experienced the reality of the risen Lord. Sometimes falls can become redemptive experiences.

Life is like a treadmill. Webster defines treadmill as "a wearisome or monotonous routine, resembling continuous activity." In other words, a treadmill gives you a lot of motion, but you never get anywhere. Perhaps this symbolized the early weeks and months in a retirement community: a lot of motion going nowhere. Perhaps I was trying to forget what I had given up by being too busy and involved.

My frantic need to establish a new life in this community had obscured a greater need—patience to discern God's presence and help. While my fall on the treadmill embarrassed me, it was a redemptive experience. It made me realize that I needed to slow down, get in touch with priorities, and acknowledge that God would show me the way.

God of the fallen , when life collapses around us, your loving arms pick us up and help us begin again. Grant us patience not to rush things but to wait for your way. Amen.

21 LOOKING OUT, LOOKING IN

Read Joshua 4:1-14

> So the Israelites did as Joshua commanded them. They took twelve stones from the middle of the Jordan, according to the number of the tribes of the Israelites, . . . and they carried them over with them to their camp, where they put them down. . . . And they are there to this day.
>
> JOSHUA 4:8-9 (NIV)

It seems an odd to take twelve stones from the middle of the Jordan River and place them at Gilgal (circle of stones). But these stones commemorate the crossing of the Jordan River. Joshua knows this act symbolizes God leading them to the land of promise. The stones will encourage successive generations to remember.

Many older people depend on physical objects to remind them of home. I chose several objects and brought them with me to remind me of my past. An old, wooden Communion set from France; a few of my prized Cooperstown baseball hats; and a ceramic cat that belonged to my sister—all reminded me of my past. When I look at them and other mementos, I often choke back the tears. My sister gave me the ceramic cat shortly before her death from cancer.

In our independent apartments, some residents place mementos of their past outside their door. One man, who spent some time in Baghdad, Iraq, placed a Muslim prayer rug outside his door. Another resident from England set an old flower vase on the shelf outside her door.

People who have Alzheimer's disease or dementia deeply appreciate having mementos of their homes in their rooms. For some it might be fading pictures of their wedding or photos of children and grandchildren. Some even have pictures of their pets, which they point to with great joy. One resident always enjoyed showing me photo albums of his cat. Another man had been a scout for the Chicago White Sox, and fascinating photos and signed autographs of baseball stars lined the wall of his room.

Recently I visited two residents in assisted living who provided a stark contrast of their relationship to their new lifestyle. One woman had six stuffed animals staring out the window of her room. She told me, "Those animals remind me how much I would love to be back in my home, and how I long to get out of here." Another resident had stuffed animals that all faced into her apartment. She said, "I love my animals. As they look at my apartment, they remind me of how fortunate I am to be here!"

What a difference in perspective. As I continued to struggle with my own regrets about leaving home, I could identify with the unhappy woman who wanted to return home. But the peace and quiet acceptance of the other resident spoke to me.

The Israelites placed those stones in the Jordan River to remind them of their history. But the time had come to move on. Hopefully, that time would come for me.

God, I am in turmoil. At times I look back to what has gone. I want to look forward to what this new life can mean. Help me. Amen.

22 COMPACTED SPACE, EXPANDED SOUL

Read Psalm 18:16-24

Answer me when I call, O God of my right!
　　You gave me room when I was in distress.

　The LORD was my support.
He brought me out into a broad place;
　　he delivered me, because he delighted in me.

PSALM 4:1; 18:18-19

Psychologists claim that anxiety comes in two forms: compacted and expanded. Compacted anxiety arises from having to live in small space, to be boxed in and confined.

During my first weeks here I suffered from "compacted anxiety." Having lived in a large home, I found the small apartment constraining. As a writer, I especially missed the expanse I had in the basement for writing. I could spread out my work, pull endless books from shelves, and revel in the wonder of so much space.

Now, it was totally different. In these tight quarters I felt like I was back in a dormitory room. (No wonder I had dreams of being back in college or seminary.) The remnants of my library were crowded onto shelves or locked up in the storage unit. Life had dwindled to minute space, and I felt closed in.

I read the Psalms once again, always food for the soul. We don't know the story of the author of Psalm 4, but apparently he is boxed in by his enemies. "You gave me room when I was in distress . . . ." he writes. Likewise the author of Psalm

18 knew "compacted space," but the Lord brought him into a broad place.

I recall one of our neighbors down the hall saying to us when we first arrived, "I know it's hard, but you'll get used to it." I doubted that! How could I ever get used to such cramped space? I know one thing: you have to have a good marriage to live in a retirement community. The limited space means you and your spouse live in close quarters.

God "gave me room when I was in distress." It took time, but soon I grew accustomed to the smaller space. I still pined for my former study. We visited another retired minister in a sister retirement community, and he had a big room for his study with a spectacular view. I admit I envied his space, but I learned to accept what I had.

My wife challenged me to write in these cramped quarters, which I considered impossible. However, with the computer hooked up, I began to keep a daily journal. Writing resumed. I learned it's not the space that matters but the will. As I began to write my journal, I began to mull over the idea of a book describing the first year in a retirement community. A search showed that nothing in that genre existed. I could write this book not as a learned observer but as an insider who was experiencing this major life transition.

Furthermore, the compacted space had created more room for my soul in two ways. It caused less stress in caring for a house and my postretirement career and more time for reflection and prayer. It also forced me to leave the apartment, to get out into the community, and to talk with residents. All this led to what came later.

No more "compacted anxiety," although the small space continued. Now, expanded soul. It reminded me of Jesus' words, "For what is a man [or woman] profited if he [she] shall gain the whole world, and lose his [her] own soul?" (Matt. 16:26, KJV). God does move in mysterious ways!

Help me realize, O surprising God, how you use small things to accomplish your purposes for our lives. Amen.

23 WHEN REALITY
REPLACES FANTASY

Read Matthew 16:21-28

> From that time Jesus began to show to His disciples that
> He must go to Jerusalem, and suffer many things . . . , and
> be killed, and be raised again the third day. Then Peter
> took Him aside and began to rebuke Him, saying, "Far be
> it from You, Lord; this shall not happen to You!"
>
> MATTHEW 16:21-22 (NKJV)

Peter can hardly believe what he has heard. Moments before
he has been the disciple who made the great confession that
Jesus is *the* Messiah. Jesus has blessed him for this marvelous
insight. Then, like a cacophony of sound, Peter hears Jesus
talking about his death in Jerusalem. Peter has perhaps fan-
tasized that Jesus will go to Jerusalem as victor not victim.
Surely he would establish the messianic kingdom and restore
Davidic glory and power to Israel.

The disciples do not get it until much later. James and
John want the best places, sitting on Jesus' right and left hand
in his glory. (Read Mark 10:35-45.) All the disciples quarrel
in the upper room the night before Jesus' crucifixion. Rivalry
exists among them as to which of them should be considered the greatest. (See Luke 22:24.) Even after the Resurrec-
tion, they don't get it. They ask the risen Christ, "Lord, is this
the time when you will restore the kingdom to Israel?" (Acts
1:6). Their fantasies of a worldly kingdom of power and glory
have to be replaced with the stark reality of a kingdom of
suffering, loss, and, for them, cruel martyrdom.

I came to this retirement community with all manner of fantasies. This would be a wonderful new life with no problems or stresses. I could finally escape the rat race of stressful living and find that elusive rocking chair. I could put my life on cruise control and ride it out for the rest of my years. How wrong I was.

Reality soon set it. The novelty wore off, and I discovered that while there are *some* similarities between life in any community, there are vast differences here, especially with the issues that arise. There were interpersonal problems between residents; we discovered that some independent living residents either ignored or resented the residents in the assisted living or dementia facilities. They referred to them as "those people" and even complained when they took "our" seats at chapel or at concerts. Then, we had problems with the administration, which failed to see the need for a campus manager, so that many irksome problems arose that had no one to solve them. Like Peter and the disciples, I began to realize that there would be difficulties and pain in following Christ in this place.

So I regressed and once again began asking myself such questions as, *What have I done? Why did we come here, only to exchange one set of problems for another?* As I mingled with the residents, I began to question my decision even more. My wife and I were among the youngest residents. We had expected more active people our age, but we were surrounded by frail people in a community where the average age was eighty-two! I began tormenting myself with an idiotic question: "Is there any way we can go back?" But there was no turning back.

Peter later discovered that following Christ meant denial of himself and taking up his cross daily, and that realization also came to me. The early excitement, the fantasies, had disappeared. I knew I faced some tough times ahead as I set my face to go to Jerusalem.

All-wise God, you have called me here. Sometimes I question that call. All I ask is that I have the mind of Christ, who emptied himself of personal gain and was obedient to death. Let me die to my ego and in dying to my fantasies accept the reality of where I am. Amen.

REFLECTIVE EXERCISES

- Think about some of the major decisions you have made in your life, such as career choice, marriage partner, relocation. Did you ever have second thoughts about those decisions? If you did, what did you do?

- Can you recall moments in your life when you felt trapped between two good decisions? What were your options? How did you make that choice?

- You have been accepted into a retirement community as a resident in independent living. The director of marketing tells you that space is limited; if you don't enter the community, you might lose that space. On the other hand, your broker informs you that your long-term care policy can afford limited home care when that becomes necessary. What decision do you make and why?

- Write the names of three persons who have been good friends with you in the community where you lived. You move into a retirement community, and only one of those persons maintains any contact with you. Which one would you prefer to make that contact and why?

- When have you experienced dreams and fantasies about your work or marriage or children that failed to materialize? How did you handle that reality?

DISCERNING MY LIFE NOW

After Six Months

Discernment offers insights into our actions and suggests new avenues to grace. It is not usually a blinding flash. . . . Discernment is a growing light, a growing awareness, a growing confidence both in God and ourselves.[8]

—PAUL WILKES

24 DISCERNING GOD'S CALL

Read 1 Samuel 3:10-21

> Now the LORD came and stood there, calling as before, "Samuel! Samuel!" And Samuel said, "Speak, for your servant is listening." Then the LORD said to Samuel, "See, I am about to do something in Israel that will make both ears of anyone who hears of it tingle."
>
> 1 SAMUEL 3:10-11

It is a moment of crisis for ancient Israel. Weak leadership by an old man, whose worthless sons are using the priestly office for their own gain, has brought the people to the verge of disaster. In that moment God calls the young man Samuel, who finally discerns that the voice in the night is God calling him to ministry.

It was a crucial moment for me too. After moaning about my life and the little time left, I decided to stop worrying about the time left and concentrate on making the right choices for whatever time did remain. Discerning God's call is never easy. Discernment is another part of detachment. We consider our life from a critical distance and then take the next step. I was bound to do just that. In the words of John Henry Newman's hymn, "I do not ask to see the distant scene; one step enough for me." But what was that step?

I distanced myself from my busyness and preoccupations and took time to listen for God's will. There is a precious internal voice that speaks to us about our lives. Samuel heard it, and so can we. We ignore this voice at our own peril.

Irritating nuisances and distractions are always present. Petty squabbles, disagreements with the corporation, and other problems continue to squelch God's call. I thought of the words from the Song of Solomon, "Catch us the foxes, the little foxes, that ruin the vineyards—for our vineyards are in blossom" (2:15).

I shelved all these distractions and through endless walks around the community and long night struggles I sought to hear God's call. I discerned that God was calling me to use all the experiences and gifts of my former ministry in this place. This place? Yes, right here where people at all stages of aging need comfort and support. It was indeed a moment of truth.

I had heard the internal voice and responded in faith. It is easy to hear other voices: others', my own; but I was sure God was calling me. Such a call comes rarely and cannot be dismissed. I will never forget this moment. As I walked the halls, I hummed to myself the words of a hymn:

Here I am, Lord. Is it I, Lord?
I have heard you calling in the night.
I will go, Lord, if you lead me.
I will hold your people in my heart.

This became my prayer. May it be yours!

25 REMEMBERING LIFE'S GRACE MOMENTS

Read Genesis 28:10-22

Then Jacob woke from his sleep and said, "Surely the LORD is in this place—and I did not know it!" And he was afraid, and said, "How awesome is this place!"

GENESIS 28:16-17

When Jacob wakes from his dream at Bethel, he is filled with fear at the awe of his experience. Only then does he realize that God is in that place. I am sure that as you grow older, you look back at your life story and realize God was there, even if you did not realize it at the time.

As I grow older and live with many older people in this community, I become painfully aware of short-term memory loss. For years I prided myself on my amazing memory. I could rattle off baseball trivia and recall the names of players from 1939 to the present. I could cite chapter and verse of most Bible stories, to the amazement of my colleagues.

Now I find myself forgetting names, faces of people, telephone numbers, and even biblical facts. I am like the man who said, "I am always forgetting three things. Names, faces and I can't remember the third thing!" Short-term memory loss is a fact of life for older people and does not mean we suffer from Alzheimer's. However, if we forget what a telephone or Bible is, that is a different matter. We cannot store information for a long time. Think of it as an address book or computer that contains a lifetime of information—but without enough room for new material.

But we can remember moments of our past when God was present in real ways. Lynn Huber, clinical gerontologist, author, spiritual director, and retreat and conference leader, has a favorite saying: "A coincidence is a miracle in which God wishes to remain anonymous." How true. In our later years we can scan our life story and say, "Surely God was in that place, and I didn't know it."

In 1976 I had to find a new job and faced frequent rejection because the jobs went to a younger man or woman. I had just been turned down for a social worker position at a mental hospital in another town and felt I had reached the end of my rope. I stopped by the office of a friend who just happened to be reading the evening paper. He noticed a job opening for a counselor at a community college. I applied, got the job; and my life had a new beginning as I moved to a new town. God was in that moment.

Because of that move, I met Alice Ann, the widow of a Presbyterian minister. I just happened to have written a book on death and dying and gave her a copy. I was working through a painful divorce, and our common pain gave birth to genuine intimacy that led to a second marriage. Thirty years later, I now realize that God was in that moment and opened the door for a "third day" in my life.

Unlike Jacob, I had no mystic dream of a ladder reaching to heaven with angels ascending and descending. But like Jacob, I struggled with the decision to leave home and identity to go to a strange and unknown new life in a retirement community. Now looking back on that struggle and blessed by my decision, I realize God was calling me to this new ministry where I am so much needed.

If you feel unsure of your life and unclear of where God calls you now, recollect those moments when God did lead you; and this God of constancy will show you the way. May Georg Neumark's prayer be your own:

If thou but suffer God to guide thee,
and hope in God through all thy ways,
God will give strength, whate'er betide thee,
and bear thee through the evil days.
Who trusts in God's unchanging love
builds on the rock that naught can move.

26 FINDING THAT VITAL BALANCE

Read Acts 2:37-47

They devoted themselves to the apostles' teaching and to
the fellowship, to the breaking of bread and to prayer.
Everyone was filled with awe.

ACTS 2:42-43 (NIV)

The vitality and vibrancy of the early church depended upon
its maintaining a vital balance. The members were a learning community that celebrated fellowship with one another.
They enjoyed common life in the body of Christ but also
devoted themselves to prayer. As I thought about my life in
this retirement community, I wondered if I might pattern
my life rhythm after that of the early church.

Even as we grow older, we need exposure to opportunities
for learning and expanding our minds. A group of us at the
retirement community formed a literary club to discuss chosen books; others initiated a Bible study for those who wanted
to deepen their understanding of scripture.

Being the fellowship, the *koinonia*, is at the heart of a
Christian community. Here we could be an "uncongenial fellowship," not based on human conditions but rooted in being
the family of God. Surely here, together in the aging process,
we could demonstrate the unity of Christ. With Christ at the
center of a community, there is always room for the other.

In this place of all places we could find a common life. We
live physically close to one another, share mutual woes, and
break bread together in the dining room every day. What an

opportunity to be a blessed community whose closeness grows daily. In fact, some residents deprived of transportation (except trips on the van) find their social interaction within the community.

That early church was a community of prayer. Seemly today the church is problem conscious, while the early church was power conscious. Reading the book of Acts makes us cognizant of the major role prayer played in the dynamic life of the early church.

We need to grow in that area, or life will lose its creative balance. I have been intentional about deepening my spiritual life and not allowing distractions to keep me from spiritual growth. I find the continual reading of spiritual books helpful. Although my library has been thinned out, the books I purchase deal with expanding the spiritual life.

Among my memories of spiritual places, none stands out more than Alice Ann's and my visit to the community of Iona in Scotland. I felt the quietness and peace of God and understood what the Celts meant by a "thin place"—there's not much between Iona and God. This is my dream for this community, to be a "thin place," a life where there's not much between Redstone and God.

John O'Donohue, in his book *Eternal Echoes: Celtic Reflections on Our Yearning to Belong*, articulates this dream for such a community and his words might be inscribed somewhere in this place, reflecting what we can become:

There is a Providence that brought us here and gave us to each other at this time. In and through us, a greater tapestry of creativity is being woven. . . . Behind all the seeming separation a deeper unity anchors everything.[9]

Teach us, O God, not to live in a community driven by power. Settle our flurry of activity and talk, and create a community where all are close to you and to one another. Amen.

27 SERVICE IS THE GOLDEN CORD

Read Mark 10:35-45

"Whoever wishes to become great among you must be
your servant, and whoever wishes to be first among you
must be slave of all."

MARK 10:43-44

After nine months of life in a retirement community, different groups of residents come into focus. Some are the Loners; others, the Gamesters; and a third group, the Volunteers.

The Loners prefer to stay in their own rooms and usually appear to get mail, ride the van to doctor's appointments or shopping tours, and dine in the communal dining room. They rarely interact with others in the community, except to exchange a few pleasantries as they pass in the hall. Striding down the halls, you hear their television sets blaring into the night. At times their frailty forces this kind of existence.

The Gamesters live to play. They view a retirement community as a place for fun and games. Most still drive their own cars and savor the freedom of doing as they please. They engage in endless card games; and if you walk down the halls at night, you can often spot them deeply engrossed in poker or blackjack or bridge. They also enjoy excursions out of the community. One woman told me she had raised six children, and when she came to this community, she planned to retire and really live. A man told me, "When I retired, I didn't do anything, and that didn't start until afternoon." Another woman said, "I have problems with this place being a convalescent home or a convent. I came here to have a good time."

The Volunteers comprise a smaller group of residents who devote hours to the life of the community. Some deliver mail; others work in the gift shop. One man uses the woodworking shop to make objects for the community; some plant flowers and beautify the grounds. Others serve on the Resident Council or drive residents to doctor's appointments. Still others serve on the religious life committee, leading daily devotionals, visiting the sick or leading sing-alongs with dementia residents.

James and John wanted chief seats in the kingdom Jesus would establish. But Jesus said the only way to greatness in his kingdom was through service. As the suffering servant who continuously poured out his life for others and washed the grimy feet of the disciples the night before he died, he set the example for all of us.

I will take time to be alone but avoid being lonely. I will try to reach out to those who remain isolated from the community. I will always have time for play because leisure is a vital necessity at any stage of life. By my example, I will try to show those preoccupied with fun and games that a greater depth of life exists through service to others. All human beings need to participate in something greater than themselves. We all want to believe we are needed and that our presence makes a difference.

James and John had to learn that "service is the golden cord close binding humankind." Their clamor for power and the easy life would soon be turned into lives given for others. Each played a major role in the life of early Christianity.

I had discerned God's will for my life, and it meant service to the community. We all can be ministers as we live out Jesus' words, "The Son of Man came not to be served but to serve" (Matt. 20:28).

Servant Lord, give us grace to follow in your footsteps where we are. Amen.

28 THE SAVING GRACE OF LAUGHTER

Read Psalm 126

A cheerful heart is good medicine,
 but a crushed spirit dries up the bones.

There is a time for everything,
. . . .
 a time to laugh.

Proverbs 17:22 (NIV); Ecclesiastes 3:1, 4 (NIV)

It was a rather dismal day at the Coffee Klatch. Everyone sat around in silence or stared out the window. One of the residents broke the silence with this story. She returned to her apartment late at night, only to find her door unlocked. Somewhat fearful, she searched her apartment and found no intruder. The next day she solved the mystery.

A resident had gone for dialysis, and a maintenance man had returned him to the woman's apartment. The man looked around and exclaimed, "My goodness! My wife has bought all new furniture." Dismayed, he decided to go into the den and slump into his favorite recliner, only to discover it was gone! After a while it dawned on him that the maintenance man had taken him to the wrong apartment! When he returned to his own place, he sat in his chair and heaved a sign of relief. Everyone had a great laugh at that story, and soon others in the room were telling their own comical stories.

The writer of Proverbs said it well, "A cheerful heart is good medicine." Laughter works like medicine in our systems. Scientists have discovered that laughter is a form of internal jogging that releases endorphins and reduces stress.

Laughter has a lot of religious connotations. It began in the Bible with two old people, Abraham and Sarah, laughing when God told them they would have a child at their advanced age. I can hear them cracking up and saying, "Our child will be born in the geriatric ward and Medicare will pay the bill." But they laughed themselves into history and named the child Isaac, which means "laughter."

G. K. Chesterton wrote, "Angels can fly because they take themselves so lightly." I learned that a sense of humor is a saving grace in my new life in this community. When I could laugh with others and at myself, it redeemed the day. I manage to get a good laugh every day in the life of this community. One ninety-year-old man told me that he had to be careful because he was paying for his cemetery plot on the installment plan. Another resident added, "I'm ninety-four. I've lived so long, my friends in heaven will think I didn't make it."

Leading a sing-along with Alzheimer's residents, I was trying to draw them into the experience. We were about to sing the song, "By the light of the silvery moon, I want to spoon." Facetiously I asked, "Why do you need a spoon by the light of the silvery moon?" Whereupon one female resident jumped from her seat and kissed me, saying, "That's what it means to spoon." Over thirty residents burst into laughter. Sad faces broke into smiles. It was a grace moment.

As I began to find my place in this new life, I realized that a sense of humor was critical. Jesus loved to laugh. We find touches of humor in many of his parables and sayings. I am sure he must have laughed heartily in the home of Mary, Martha, and Lazarus, appropriately called "House of Laughter."

Laughter is a ray of sunshine piercing a dark and overcast sky and bringing us into the presence of God. It is saving grace in a retirement community.

Lord, help me to laugh at myself and with others. Amen.

29 THE BLESSING OF GRANDCHILDREN

Read Psalm 128

The LORD bless you from Zion.
 May you see the prosperity of Jerusalem
  all the days of your life.
 May you see your children's children.

PSALM 128:5-6

Living with older people often means you miss contact with the younger generation. We always enjoy conversing and joking with the high-school kids who serve us in the dining hall. But in a community of older people, we rarely see children. Ever so often, grandchildren or great-grandchildren visit and become the center of attention.

My wife and I are blessed with being near two granddaughters: Brannon, age seven, and ReidAnn, age five. We have become part of their lives, attending their school functions, watching them play baseball and soccer, and going to other activities. Their love of life and contagious enthusiasm always give us a lift and bring joy into our lives.

Some time ago I was presenting lectures at the Presbyterian Home in Summerville, South Carolina. Our grandchildren came to eat lunch with us. Grandson Daniel, who was then three years old, glanced around the room, saw all the white-haired elders, and exclaimed, "I never saw so many grandmas and grandpas in all my life." I was mortified, but the residents loved it.

Some of the residents live far from grandchildren or have no grandchildren of their own. But I watch as they fall all over the young children who visit. A group of residents hopes to initiate a foster-grandparent program with our new library, where residents can read to young children and reach across the generations. A unique affinity exists between them.

One of my great concerns about retirement communities is *geriatric segregation*. We need to bring the generations together, for each can learn much from the other. The new library will help us begin to span the gap.

The psalmist's prayer, "May you see your children's children" has been answered for my wife and me. Although eight of our grandchildren are scattered across the country, now we have close contact with two little girls. We are part of their lives and share with their parents their growth toward maturity. But my heart goes out to other older people here who have no grandchildren or rarely see them. Not all are like one male resident who now has seventeen great-grandchildren with another on the way.

When we had been here a few weeks, I was showing my grandchildren my library with its new shelves. ReidAnn exclaimed, "Gramps, you have one groovy setup here!" One of my best moments came when Brannon played her violin for residents with Alzheimer's disease. Grandchildren are a gift from God and bring joy and love into our lives!

God, you love us unconditionally and bring daily grace into our lives. We thank you that a special part of that love is given to us by grandchildren. May we always be grateful for them. Amen.

REFLECTIVE EXERCISES

- Recall times in your life when you sought God's will. What was your experience?

- Draw a line across a white sheet of paper. At the left margin write the year you were born. At the right margin speculate the year you will die. Put the present date where it belongs on the line. How much time do you have left? What do you want to do with the remaining time of your life?

- Write a brief note on how you would spend a day with no responsibilities, simply free to be and do as you want.

- If you lived in a retirement community, how would you spend your time?

- At what times in your life has a sense of humor saved the day?

- Fantasize a community where older people and young people live together.

FINDING COMMUNITY

Months Seven to Nine

We are bound together because we have begun to realize that a part of our work as members of the Body of Christ is to honor one another's attempts to be faithful, recognizing our brotherhood even as we acknowledge our differences.[10]

—Robert Benson

30 A HOUSE DIVIDED

Read Ephesians 2:11-22

"Every kingdom divided against itself is laid waste, and
no city or house divided against itself will stand."

MATTHEW 12:25

At my first chapel service I made an interesting observation.
The independent living residents sat on one side of the
chapel, and assisted living residents sat on the other side—
a kind of segregation. The chapel was divided not by age or
race or gender but by stage of aging.

Later, as I talked with some of the volunteers in assisted
living, I learned the division was not accidental, nor was it
confined to the chapel. Some in independent living complained when they had to return "those people" who had
wandered from familiar surroundings back to their area.

This division bothered me. Because I had worked as a
chaplain in nursing homes, I felt a closeness to people who
suffer from Alzheimer's disease or other forms of dementia.
Having been with them, I knew they needed affirmation not
rejection, warm hugs not cold shoulders.

Jesus' words "No city or house divided against itself will
stand" were quoted by Abraham Lincoln when he ran for
the Senate in 1858. He referred to the major conflict between
the North and the South that threatened to divide the nation.

The church at Ephesus was urged to break down walls of
division, for in a Christian community, "You are no longer
strangers and aliens, but you are citizens with the saints and
also members of the household of God" (Eph. 2:19). God's

community does not allow for exclusion based on race, gender, economic situation, or health issues.

At one chapel service Edwin Markham's poem "Outwitted" came to mind:

> He drew a circle that shut me out—
> Rebel, heretic, a thing to flout.
> But Love and I had the wit to win:
> We drew a circle that took him in.[11]

Our community at times more closely resembled a square of division than a circle of love. Breaking down this dividing wall became one of my passions. I began sitting with the assisted living folks in the chapel, and soon a few independent living residents followed suit. I worked hard to help assisted living and dementia residents feel that they were part of the community.

On our communal bulletin board I noted a message about crayons. Some crayons are sharp; some are dull. Some are pretty, and some are not. Some have weird names, but all are different colors. They exist nicely in the same box.

This community represents many ethnic groups. We seem to relate well to one another across these barriers that could separate us. But we will never be a community until we become the circle of love, the box of assorted crayons. What an opportunity we have to be that community in this place where we share so much common life!

Loving Parent, forgive us for making distinctions and avoiding people who differ from us. May we see your image in every old person, regardless of frailty and embrace him or her as we would welcome Christ. Amen.

31 BECOMING A CARING COMMUNITY

Read 1 Corinthians 12:12-27

> So God has put the body together in such a way that extra honor and care are given to those parts that have less dignity. This makes for harmony among the members, so that all the members care for each other equally.
>
> 1 CORINTHIANS 12:24-25 (NLT)

During my first months as a new resident in this retirement community I spent time trying to figure out what kind of a community this was. I quietly observed life. My initial impression was that some people treat this setting like a casino, playing cards several nights a week and even in the afternoons. This activity becomes the focus of their community life.

For others this community has become a church away from home. Unless residents can get to their "home" church, this retirement center becomes their church. Local congregations seemingly make little effort to transport residents to church or involve them in congregational life. Visits by local pastors are rare events.

However, this faith-based retirement community has a unique opportunity to care for those within. Everyone needs to belong and be liberated from the exile of loneliness. Frank MacEowen writes, "In the world of the sleepwalkers intimacy is all too often replaced by anonymity. Many people let years pass without letting others know them deeply. They are just as homeless in their inner lives as people living in cardboard boxes on the street."[12]

When Saul of Tarsus was knocked off his high horse on the Damascus Road, he heard a voice say, "Saul, Saul, why do you persecute me?" When Saul answered, "Who are you, Lord?" the answer came, "I am Jesus, whom you are persecuting." Saul had never harmed the historic Jesus, but in harming Jesus' followers, he was attacking the Christ. Writing to a divided Corinthian congregation, Paul explains the unity of the church using images of the body. In a Christian community every member is indispensable. The involvement of every member is essential for the well-being of the whole.

Furthermore, "extra honor and care are given to those parts that have less dignity" (1 Cor. 12:24, NLT), resulting in a unity among all members. "If one member suffers, all suffer together with it; if one member is honored, all rejoice together with it" (1 Cor. 12:26). In a Christian retirement community extra honor and care should be given to the frail and those suffering from Alzheimer's disease or other forms of dementia. In a Christian community when one resident goes to the hospital or faces some form of suffering, every member is in pain. Conversely, when one member is honored, there is no jealousy or envy. Cooperation rather than competition prevails.

There is a basic difference between community and conformity. Conformity requires us to be like everyone else, leaving us with no identity of our own. Community affirms our individuality and nourishes us to be ourselves in a community that accepts our right to be different.

We have a unique opportunity to be a Christian community in this place. Pockets of division need to be eradicated; there is work to be done if we are to be a caring community.

But I feel a compelling call to work for that blessed community where every person is loved and affirmed and a unity exists that is often not found elsewhere.

God, who at the beginning of time said, "It is not good that the man should be alone," help us to make this a true community of love. Amen.

32 A SENSE OF APPRECIATION FOR ALL

Read Philippians 1:1-11

I thank my God every time I remember you.

PHILIPPIANS 1:3

Unlike letters of admonition or correction to other churches that Paul founded, Paul has only words of appreciation for the Christians at Philippi. Their partnership in the gospel has brought constant joy to his heart.

You cannot live in a retirement community like Redstone without feeling a deep sense of debt to those whose vision made the community possible and to the staff and residents who serve us here. I am debtor to those who had the vision and energy to make this community a reality where a continuum of care exists. I am debtor to those who established a benevolent fund that ensures a place for all, even if funds are exhausted, until death comes.

Despite some infrequent criticisms (usually about the food or policies of the administration), the prevailing attitude here is a genuine sense of gratitude for life in the community. I can recount many instances of kindness to me. Once in the dining room I slipped and spilled my dinner everywhere. I felt terribly embarrassed, but one of our young servers immediately came to my rescue. Without hesitation he assured me that it was an accident and proceeded to clean up my mess and replace the soiled tablecloth.

One of our friends fell and broke his hip. For a while he will live in assisted living, hoping to return to his apartment one day. Every morning he comes in his wheelchair to put his copy of *USA Today* in our mailbox. You don't forget these random acts of kindness.

Another friend down the hall, an avid reader of books, often loans me some of his books, knowing my library has grown smaller and smaller. A member of the nursing staff saves me an endless amount of time by giving me allergy shots every week. Our able receptionist always keeps me aware of hospitalized residents and goes the second mile in listening to my concerns.

I have a special affinity for our maintenance personnel, who have the unenviable task of taking care of one hundred and forty apartments. Whenever a physical need arises related to an apartment, they come quickly and fix the problem with a cheerful manner. Other residents, knowing my love of humor, swap stories with me, and often their stories brighten what could have been some dismal days. When I had to undergo surgery and spend a lot of time confined to my apartment, many residents showed their concern and remembered me in prayer.

Redstone is a not-for-profit, continuing care retirement community. We may lack the luxuries and niceties that other retirement communities have, but the spirit of helpfulness creates a hospitality not always found in such communities. Is it any wonder that such grace compels me to volunteer for others, a small way to give back the goodness shown me?

Loving God, we thank you for the goodness and acts of kindness that surround our lives. May our thanksgiving be thanks living. Amen.

33 WHEN GOSSIP IS GOOD

Read Proverbs 12

Some people make cutting remarks,
    but the words of the wise bring healing.

Timely advice is as lovely as golden apples
    in a silver basket.

PROVERBS 12:18; 25:11 (NLT)

Let's set the record straight. Say the word *gossip* and immediately we think of someone who spreads malicious slander and rips people apart. Granted, some people do enjoy talking about other people's faults and nibbling at their reputations. They seem to relish juicy tidbits about the scandals and disgraces of others. By tearing others down, they build themselves up.

The book of James has much to say about the evils of the tongue. The recent fires in southern California created havoc and destroyed homes. So James reminds us, "How great a forest is set ablaze by a small fire. And the tongue is a fire" (James 3:5-6).

Yet the word *gossip* originally had a positive meaning. If you look it up in a dictionary, you will find its origins in the words *God* and *sibling*. *Godsibb* in some British dialects is the word for godparent, a person who sponsors a child at baptism.

Gossip can be a holy thing when it serves to communicate concern for other people. Gossip is a form of social bonding. Our common life here demands we be compassionate to those who are hurt and broken.

Words can be a source of healing, and this is particularly true in a retirement community. We live daily in the midst of sorrow, sadness, and trouble. Sharing concerns with others is a positive use of gossip to promote awareness of need.

One of the most creative initiatives taken by the residents was the development of a daily television broadcast called *Good Morning, Neighbors* that airs over our closed-circuit television channel. Not only do we give announcements for the community and share some devotional thoughts, but the program alerts residents as to who is in the hospital. Many residents watch this program religiously because it keeps them informed of neighbors in need. As an outgrowth of this form of good gossip, residents call, send cards, and visit their friends.

I do not deny that some retirement communities have what I call their "clackety-clack" clubs. Members always manage to find something wrong and are never pleased. They also seem to revel in talking about other residents. They need to be mindful of Jesus' words to Peter, when he asked about John, and Jesus replied, "If it is my will that he remain until I come, what is that to you? Follow me!" (John 21:22).

But we need to reinvent the word *gossip* and acknowledge the power and significance of sharing information about other people that is helpful and kind. I find little of the negative here in this community. What I do find is genuine concern for the welfare of other residents and gossip that passes on information in a kind way.

It may well take many years to change people's understanding of the word *gossip*. The negative meaning seems to live on. Will Rogers mentioned it when he said, "Try to live

your life so that you wouldn't be afraid to sell the family par-
rot to the town gossip."

In this retirement community we *do* gossip but seldom
with cutting remarks or cruel words. We share helpful information in order to show kindness and compassion.

Lord, help me to gossip with a filter of love on my lips.
Amen.

34 IT TAKES A VILLAGE

Read John 12:1-9

Now a certain man was ill, Lazarus of Bethany, the village of Mary and her sister Martha....

Six days before the Passover Jesus came to Bethany, the home of Lazarus, whom he had raised from the dead.

JOHN 11:1; 12:1

After leaving his home in Nazareth, Jesus becomes an itinerant preacher with no permanent home. "'Foxes have holes, and birds of the air have nests; but the Son of Man has nowhere to lay his head'" (Luke 9:58). There was a special place where Jesus enjoyed hanging out—Bethany, the home of Lazarus and his sisters, Mary and Martha.

We know that Jesus often stayed there; he went there six days before the Passover and journeyed back and forth from that village to Jerusalem during his last week on earth. Each morning, from Sunday to Wednesday, during Holy Week, Jesus got up and walked from Bethany to Jerusalem.

My imagination takes me to that village of Bethany where Jesus stayed with good friends and walked its lanes. Visiting his friends at Bethany enabled Jesus to know this village well. I am sure he not only spent time with his friends in the village but often sauntered through the town, stopping to speak to strangers or responding to their needs.

For many years I lived in a small town in North Carolina. Every day during my postretirement years, I would make my rounds. I would chat with people outside the post office, stop by the library and the bookstore. Sometimes I would saunter down the main streets of the village and sit on a bench near the courthouse, talking with colorful characters who parked there all day.

After many months of living in *this* community, my wife helped me realize that this is a village too. We have similar places in this small village: a bank, a gift shop, a library, and medical office are all within walking distance. Now I wander down the halls of this "village" and often stop to speak to staff in the front office or residents I meet or the bank teller. While much more restricted in space, it still has all the characteristics of a small village.

When I went through surgery and was confined to the campus, I found joy in daily walks. I would talk with residents who sat in the lobby. On pretty days I would venture outside and listen to the conversation of new friends who sat on the benches.

One evening I went outside where some assisted living residents had gathered to watch the sunset. As I listened to them express their pain and isolation, I realized how small my problems were in contrast to theirs. Later I visited with independent living residents in the mail room. It is amazing how the mail room becomes a place for conversation and encounters. Suddenly I felt transported to my former village in North Carolina, stopping outside the post office and talking with friends.

For Jesus, Bethany meant much: a place to kick off his sandals and relax with his friends, a village where he felt at home. For me, it takes a village to feel at home. I would have a difficult time living in a cold, unfriendly apartment complex in the city where often no one knows a neighbor. Here, I still have a village.

God of our inner lives, help me realize that I am not confined to the space where I live but can walk the halls of this village. Amen.

35 WHERE DEATH IS NO STRANGER

Read John 14:1-6

We know that when this earthly tent we live in is taken down—when we die and leave these bodies—we will have a home in heaven, an eternal body made for us by God . . . and not by human hands.

2 CORINTHIANS 5:1 (NLT)

During our first year here, fifteen residents died. Death is no stranger in a retirement community. Every month we have a memorial service; only once was the service omitted because no one had died. In a close community we all feel the power of John Donne's words, "Any man's [woman's] death diminishes me, because I am involved in [hu]mankind."

Sometimes residents die in their apartments after short stays in a hospital. Some have died in the hospital. One resident died in the dining room! Another resident, while broadcasting over our closed-circuit television, suffered a massive stroke and died three days later. Some residents have called in hospice, those angels of mercy who bring compassionate care. We miss our friends and mourn their loss. Their departure leaves a void in the life of the community.

Our lives stretch out before us as a long highway filled by the column of a marching band. Suddenly one or more of the players drops out, never to be seen again. The sad truth is that often their places are not filled. Even when new residents come to take their apartments, memories of our departed friends haunt us. Life is never the same.

In a famous book on anatomy used in the Middle Ages are the words *Mors Ultima Linea Rerum Est*—"Death is everything's final limit." Death writes the last line of every person's book of life, and that awesome finality is no more keenly felt than in a retirement community.

Even if we try to deny the reality of our death and distract ourselves from its nearness with endless activities, it is always present. The death of someone in the community brings to mind our own demise.

A few months ago I visited a resident in the hospital who was on kidney dialysis. He said, "In a matter of months, some of my friends at the dialysis center have died. I just hope I can make it until May when my son from California comes to visit us." He didn't make it. His pain became so great he stopped the dialysis, came back to his apartment here, and died with dignity while listening to his children sing on the community's closed-circuit television.

Death is always present here. In Margaret Craven's touching novel *I Heard the Owl Call My Name*, a young priest learns from the Native Americans of the Northwest their belief that when a person is going to die, the owl calls his or her name. The owl has called many of our residents by name, and others will be called. One day the owl will call my name.

In this community, where death is no stranger, where loss of friends becomes a regular reality, we must prepare for our death by living each day to the fullest. We express gratitude for knowing that "when this earthly tent we live in is taken down . . . we will have a home in heaven."

Others may deny death, O God; but living here, we cannot. So we make our peace with death and live each day as if there were no tomorrow. Amen.

REFLECTIVE EXERCISES

- When in your life have you felt excluded or on the edge of things, like a child never picked to be on a team or a college student never selected for a fraternity or sorority or a candidate losing a desired job to another? How did that experience of exclusion make you feel?

- Imagine a community that excludes no one. What would such a community look like?

- When have you been ministered to by someone who has been excluded? How did you feel about this experience?

- What experiences have you had of being part of a caring community? How did that differ from being an outsider?

- A resident in a nursing home says to you, "Why has the Lord left me here so long? I am of no value to anyone." How do you respond to her?

MINISTRY TO OTHERS

Last Months of the Year

It is now time for you to receive your new gift. It is time for you to listen and to hear the gift of God's call, for God is calling you by name, calling you as Abraham and Sarah were called in their very late life, . . . calling you to a new life of creative loving.[13]

—Jane Marie Thibault

36 GOD CALLS IN A RETIREMENT COMMUNITY

Read Exodus 3:1-15

> When the LORD saw that he had gone over to look, God called to him from within the bush, "Moses! Moses!" . . .
> "So now, go. I am sending you to Pharaoh to bring my people the Israelites out of Egypt."
>
> EXODUS 3:4, 10 (NIV)

God calls Moses at the age of eighty to lead the Israelites out of Egypt. It is an awesome task. No wonder Moses replies, "Who am I, that I should go to Pharaoh and bring the Israelites out of Egypt?" At his ripe old age Moses deserves to retire with his family in Midian and enjoy his later years. But in his later years, God calls.

The cliche is that retired persons are more interested in entitlement than involvement, more concerned with pleasure than service. While retirement living tends to segregate the retired into separate communities, God calls us to ministry right there.

It is a pitfall of living in a retirement community that we withdraw into ourselves and become preoccupied with our own pains and pleasures. If we do not reach out to others, we become like tops spinning endlessly around ourselves.

While we may not experience an awesome call like Moses' at the "far side of the desert," God does call in our later years. Some residents continue to volunteer in their churches or offer time to charitable organizations in the community. One place to hear God's call is within the retirement community.

In a Christian community, everyone is a minister. I am the only ordained minister living here; but every resident is a minister, called by God to minister to others. Living in this area has made me appreciate even more the work of Fred Rogers. He made *Mr. Rogers' Neighborhood* his ministry. As he wrote, "Ministry doesn't have to be only through a church or even through an ordination. And I think we all can minister to others in this world by being compassionate and caring."[14]

I find my deep gladness in helping residents in this community. I feel a special calling to those who have dementia or Alzheimer's disease. Often they are marginalized and live apart from the life of the community. So I volunteer time in providing worship for those often bypassed, leading groups, and visiting them. They are among God's dearest children.

One of my favorite hymns, written by Daniel L. Schutte, speaks of God's call and our response. For a few moments, meditate on its lyrics and ask God to show you God's call in a retirement community.

I, the Lord of sea and sky,
I have heard my people cry.

. . . .

Who will bear my light to them?
Whom shall I send?

Here I am, Lord. Is it I, Lord?
I have heard you calling in the night.
I will go, Lord, if you lead me.
I will hold your people in my heart.

Text and music © 1981, OCP Publications, 5536 NE Hassalo, Portland, OR 97213. All rights reserved. Used with permission.

37 COMPASSION KNEELS AND CARES

Read Luke 10:25-37

"Which of these three, do you think, was a neighbor to the man who fell into the hands of the robbers?" He said, "The one who showed him mercy." Jesus said to him, "Go and do likewise."

LUKE 10:36-37

Jesus' parable of the good Samaritan continues to haunt us in every age. It reminds us that God does not judge by creeds or religious performance but by deeds of love and mercy.

This story exemplifies four philosophies of life. "What's yours is mine, and I'm going to take it" is the attitude of the robbers. "What's mine is mine, and I'm going to hold on to it" reflects the response of the priest and Levite to human need. "What's mine is yours if you pay me for it" is the way the innkeeper responds. "What's mine is yours, and I give it with love" expresses the Samaritan's concern.

The priest and Levite are religious leaders who put their own safety and religious rites above human need. A Sunday school teacher asked students why these religious people passed by the hurt man. A little girl answered, "Because they saw he had already been robbed!" So often we pass by people who have nothing to give us in return.

The Samaritan was a member of a hated race, whose separation from the Jews was linked to the fall of the Northern Kingdom to the Assyrians. I am sure the disciples were shocked when Jesus made this hated outsider the hero of the story. The Samaritan had compassion on the wounded man, bound up his wounds, and followed through with his love by telling the innkeeper he would return and pay whatever costs were involved in the man's continued care.

In a retirement community, we live close to one another. On one occasion, when a power failure caused darkness to descend on our community, residents gathered on the front porch or talked in the halls, just as if they were family. But our neighbors are not simply the people who live next door to us; they are anyone in need—someone who needs a listening ear or helping hand or understanding heart. In our community, opportunities to lend a hand and heart to those wounded alongside the road of aging meet us every day.

A community is only a caring community when members are making the transition from "the community for myself" to "myself for the community," when each person's heart opens to all the others without exception.

A retirement community is far more than a place where people live under the same roof and eat in the same dining room. That is a hotel. A caring community is a place where each person looks not only to his or her own interests but also to the interests of others.

The words of a Ghanaian song point the way to a caring community,

Jesu, Jesu, fill us with your love.
Show us how to serve the neighbors we have from you.
Neighbors are rich and poor,
Varied in color and race,
Neighbors are near and far away.

Here we care about neighbors next door or down the hall or on the third floor. Here we care for all, neighbors varied in health, neighbors with memory loss or confined to wheelchairs. All are neighbors God sends to us.

Compassionate God, who showed us the way to love through Jesus, the exemplary good Samaritan, help us to be like him. May we pray this prayer, "Lord, treat me tomorrow as I treat my neighbors today." Amen.

38 A DISCERNING HEART

Read Ephesians 4:32–5:2

> Be kind to one another, tenderhearted, forgiving one
> another, as God in Christ has forgiven you.

EPHESIANS 4:32

I cannot walk down the long hallways in this community or
eat with the residents or visit with them in their rooms without feeling great compassion for them and reverence for their
stories. Everyone longs to tell his or her story to someone
and have it accepted and understood.

When God gave the new king one wish, Solomon asked for
"a discerning heart" (NIV). In a retirement community we
render no greater service to one another than in those sacred
moments when we listen as persons tell their story. Listening, without interjecting our own stories, is a gift we offer.

We initiated a weekly men's group several months ago.
Each man is in charge of the program. At first, the men
brought in other presenters. Then we begin to tell our life
stories, to chronicle our careers; and that became holy ground
for each of us.

We also receive a gift when we realize that every story is
in some way the story of us all. I have spent time straining
to understand a man in dementia care who suffers from
Parkinson's disease. Although it is difficult at times to understand his words, if I am patient, the truth comes home. Inter-
acting with Richard has evoked memories of responding to
my own mother, who had a similar condition. Although I
had spent most of my life in North Carolina, I am constantly

amazed at how I connect with the stories and sayings of people from western Pennsylvania. One lady who lives near us always responds when we ask her, "How are you?" with "I'm vertical!" I can resonate with that!

At dinner one night I simply asked a friend about his wife who suffered from profound Alzheimer's disease. For the next twenty minutes he poured out his story, relating endless agonies of her long disease, watching her fade away until she lost all identity. He retold the story of her decline into this dreaded disease and of his own pain when she no longer seems to recognize him. When he finished, he said, "Thanks for listening. At times I just have to tell someone. It helps." How many more residents like Bill are waiting for someone to listen?

When I cannot attend chapel service, I watch it on our community's closed-circuit TV system. Recently, after the service had ended, I noted two residents sitting on the front row, conversing with each other. I felt somewhat guilty about listening, but I'm glad I did.

One resident was telling her story . . . a stroke, followed by a heart attack, a recuperative stay in the hospital and then in a nursing facility, and finally a return to her apartment. Her friend Janet listened with empathy. Not once did she interrupt with her own problems (which were many). I felt I had overheard a genuine pastoral conversation! Her listener had suffered from a broken back and was on oxygen, but she never talked about herself. Sadly, this lovely woman who provided such a critical function died. The whole community mourned her loss. Janet was a minister who offered much-needed gentle concern.

Those of us who live in a retirement community and all who live elsewhere might make this our prayer:

Compassionate God, help me not to walk behind others or to walk in front of them but to walk beside them with kindness. Amen.

39 OVERCOMING FEAR OF THE "OTHER"

Read 1 John 4:7-21

There is no fear in love, but perfect love casts out fear.

1 JOHN 4:18

Every older person has fears. Those who deny these fears are fooling themselves. Some fear being robbed; others fear forms of later-life disability. Most of the residents express fears of rising rent and diminished finances. Many of our older adults fear they may develop a form of dementia and, therefore, avoid any contact with residents in dementia care.

At first I was irritated, even angry, when I sensed this attitude among a few independent living residents. Some complained when assisted living residents congregated in the lounge or wandered the halls. Often they refer to these residents as "those people." A few apartment residents seem to resent my volunteer work with Alzheimer's residents, believing I have gone "off limits."

A resident in independent living told me that she would never go "over there" to the personal care and dementia units because "we have our place, and they have theirs; and that's the way it is." I could almost read the fear on her face. However, a few residents have gone with me for worship and visitation, and now they love those moments. They tell me, "Those dear people do more for me than I do for them, and they will never know my name."

As I reflected, however, I grew calmer. After all, I had a special concern for Alzheimer's residents because my mother had died from this disease at an early age. That experience made me more compassionate toward those who suffer from it. I also had worked with Alzheimer's residents for several years as a chaplain in a nursing home that had Alzheimer's and memory impairment units. Even then I tried to crack the language code that separated us. Most of our independent living residents have no such experience in their lives.

It seemed that a lot of the avoidance and fear of our Alzheimer's residents was based on a denial of aging. To ignore their existence is rooted in the denial of the old woman or old man we will become.

In First John 4 the beloved disciple makes it clear that agape, self-giving love, is the central message of the gospel. He affirms, "There is no fear in love." When we love others with the same love with which Christ loves us, we cannot be afraid of anyone.

A few independent living residents do volunteer time with Alzheimer's residents. They play games with them, read to them, play the piano for them, and sit with them. I admit my ministry is there. I believe it is there that Christ is found.

I recall a moment of truth at one of our sing-alongs. I had changed the words of a favorite hymn, "Jesus Loves Me." When we sang the hymn in the following way, several residents who usually did not sing but sat slumped over, suddenly sat up and began to sing. Jesus loved them too!

> Jesus loves me! This I know,
> for the Bible tells me so.
> *Older ones* to him belong;
> They are weak, but he is strong.[15]

One volunteer said, "We need to be more understanding and accepting of these people. After all, we may find ourselves in this very situation." She spoke the truth.

From our blindness that cannot see the pain in others' lives, from our fears that distance us from others, from our indifference that cannot relate to others' suffering, deliver us, O God. Amen.

40 GOING OUTSIDE THE CAMP

Read Hebrews 13:7-16

> Therefore Jesus also suffered outside the city gate in order to sanctify the people by his own blood. Let us then go to him outside the camp and bear the abuse he endured.
>
> HEBREWS 13:12-13

In many retirement communities, assisted living and dementia care are "off limits." People with profound dementia are kept behind locked doors for their own safety. Particularly at sundown they are prone to wander and possibly leave the facility. Many independent living residents have never gone beyond those closed doors. One resident even called it "that place," candidly stating that he never wanted to venture there.

I recall a physician in another town who told me I was wasting my time in nursing homes: "All they need is medical care. They're out of it anyway and don't even know you are there." What a sad attitude.

A legend in the Talmud speaks of the coming of the Messiah. When Rabbi Joshua ben Levi came upon the prophet Elijah, he asked him, "When will the Messiah come?" Elijah replied, "He is at the gates of the city . . . sitting among the poor covered with wounds."

Jesus ministered to the outcasts. The religious hierarchy of his day criticized his association with tax collectors and sinners. But Christ acted out the prophecy of Isaiah, that the servant Messiah would not "break a bruised reed or quench a smoldering wick" (Matt. 12:20). I am sure that today Christ can be found in the haunting, blank faces of those souls who sit behind closed doors covered with the wounds of a terrible disease of the brain. I admit I often feel frustrated and helpless as I sit with them.

Yet, as Christians we are to go outside the camp and minister to those who are "outside their minds." At times I despair about my ministry. So often these residents, victims of "the funeral that never ends," just sit and stare at me with faces that display no recognition or emotion. But in these moments "outside the camp," I find my deepest joy and satisfaction.

I keep trying to relate to Mary who never acknowledges my presence but continues flipping pages of a magazine that she never reads. I haven't given up yet on Captain Jack, the resident with the safari hat, who usually says two or three words: "What?" "Who?" "When?" I learned from his wife that he had been a newspaper reporter, so these *W* words were still part of his brain, destroyed by semantic dementia.

I encourage Fran, a former singer, to give me a solo every time she sees me; and she beams as she breaks into some unknown aria. I sit and listen to Richard, a victim of Parkinson's disease, whose speech is garbled but whose mind is sharp as a tack. If I listen, I will hear incredible stories.

Friend and clinical geriatrician Jane Thibault has inspired me to continue this ministry. She wrote me the following:

Work with dementia patients may be your most significant contribution yet! I think the whole issue of 50 percent of folks over eighty-five becoming ill with some kind of dementia is extremely frightening, especially to baby boomers. If you can develop ways to make life meaningful and joyful for them and their caregivers (both family and staff), you will help stem the tide of mass euthanasia I see coming around the bend!

So I continue my ministry "outside the camp."

God of the lost and forsaken, may we see Christ in the people outside the camp. Amen.

41 HIDDEN ANGEL

Read Hebrews 13:1-2

Do not neglect to show hospitality to strangers, for by
that some have entertained angels without knowing it.

HEBREWS 13:2

I had never seen this person before. I was leading worship
in dementia care when I spotted her—sitting in a corner of
the room with her head bowed. She seemed so forlorn, oblivious to everything. I wondered why the aides had brought
her from her room to the worship service.

Then I heard this woman give voice to the same words
over and over again.

Angel of God, my guardian dear,
To whom God's love commits me here,
Ever this day be at my side.
To light and guard, to rule and guide.

Her frail voice sounded like a moan, as if she were crying
out for help. Only later did I realize that her words were a
prayer of Saint Augustine, which she had learned as a child
in her Roman Catholic church.

A few days later when I visited the woman, she repeated
the same prayer. I borrowed a rosary from a Catholic friend
and showed it to her, and she repeated other prayers. Once
she asked for a priest but was content for me to hear her
prayers. I assured her she was in a state of grace.

The letter to the Hebrews encourages us not only to love
one another as angels but to entertain strangers. Abraham

welcomed strangers in his tent at Hebron by the oaks of Mamre and only afterward realized his visitors were angels (Gen. 18:1-33).

For many of us, this woman who suffers from Alzheimer's disease and is now a hospice patient became an angel. The disease had robbed her of her identity and her memory. Her husband resided in assisted living. She never recognized him when he visited. Disoriented in time and space, she rarely spoke in recognizable language except for those prayers. Although the disease had ravaged her brain, she had retained pockets of religious memory from a distant childhood. These prayers, taught by a nun or priest, had lingered in her confused mind.

Sometimes people with Alzheimer's disease are denied access to worship because their behavior can be disruptive and it seems pointless when they cannot understand the liturgy. But I have worked long and hard to help them understand, singing old hymns, repeating the Twenty-Third Psalm and the Lord's Prayer, and showing them religious objects. They do understand.

I will always regard that white-haired woman, mumbling her prayers, as an angel of God. She wore no halo, but she reminded us that we should never neglect these lost souls who still cling to childhood faith. I memorized her prayer and made it my mantra.

God, you often come to us as a stranger. May we never forget that nothing, not even Alzheimer's, can separate us from the love of God. Amen.

42 CHARITY BEGINS AT HOME

Read 1 Corinthians 13

Love is patient; love is kind; love is not envious or boastful or arrogant or rude. It does not insist on its own way; it is not irritable or resentful. . . . It bears all things, believes all things, hopes all things, endures all things. Love never ends.

1 CORINTHIANS 13:4-5, 7-8

Recently as I helped some independent living residents with certain problems, I realized that opportunities for ministry surround me. The average age of residents here is eighty-one, and all of us are "aging in place." Medical and personal needs arise every day. As the only retired counselor in residence, I find my services in great demand. Many people have come to me, confiding their problems and wanting a listening ear. I know my free time has been diminished; but life is nothing more than relationships, and this is what endures.

I am a high priest forever, after the order of Melchizedek, but so is every member of the community in the priesthood of all believers. So, others join me in reaching out to residents who need care. At times it requires standing in the gap when illness comes or being a nonanxious presence when death is imminent. At other times it is little deeds of kindness such as making things in the wood shop or helping people with cars that won't start.

What I have perceived is the hunger for love, the kind of love Paul described in his letter to the Corinthian faith community. John O'Donohue expressed this universal need when he wrote, "In everyone's life, there is great need for an *anam cara*, a soul friend." With the *anam cara* you could share your innermost self. "In this love, you are understood as you are without mask or pretension. . . .Where you are understood, you are at home."[16] I envision this retirement community as a place for soul friends who offer this kind of caring love to one another.

In this community, where many battle the debilities of aging, some residents cannot offer this love. As O'Donohue expressed it, "Others want to love, to give themselves, but they have no energy. They carry around in their hearts the corpses of past relationships and are addicted to hurt as confirmation of identity."[17] But others can show the way.

A role model for an *anam cara* is my Italian friend, Woodie. He loves to tell the stories of his past, how the sister in parochial school always referred to him as "that boy on the second row," how his brother named him after President Woodrow Wilson. Woodie survived many illnesses and crises. Once he said, "They have been waiting fifty-six years to bury me; I should never have lived this long."

Woodie is his wife's *anam cara*. She suffers from profound dementia. Every day, without fail, Woodie takes her in her wheelchair all over the community. In good weather he can be seen wheeling Jackie around our walkways. He shepherds her everywhere and is her constant companion. Jackie and Woodie modeled late-life marriage, and their relationship reminds me of a Robert Sexton epigram:

Somehow the world keeps aging:
Somehow you never do;

somehow I know—in the heart of my heart—
I'll always be young with you.

Such genuine love inspires us all in this community. This eighty-nine-year-old man demonstrates what a soul friend is. If only we could show this charity to one another every day!

Christ, our true anam cara, *you showed us the way. Place some person on our heart, and help us love that person as you love us. Amen.*

43 HELP ME!

Read Acts 16:6-10

During the night Paul had a vision: there stood a man of Macedonia pleading with him and saying, "Come over to Macedonia and help us."

ACTS 16:9

"Help me, help me," he cried during worship in dementia care. A stillness hung in the air, as everyone wondered what would happen next. I walked back to where he sat and said, "I understand. We all need to help each other here." He smiled and seemed satisfied. That's all it took—affirming his cry.

Paul planned to launch a great campaign in Bithynia, right on the shores of the Black Sea, dreaming of an Asiatic empire for Christ. We know Luke had been summoned to Troas to treat Paul. Luke pled with Paul to take the gospel to Macedonia. At Troas, Paul had a vision of a man pleading with him to cross the Aegean Sea to Macedonia.

I have seen the vision of people with Alzheimer's disease pleading for help. They may not have said it with words; at times they seem indifferent to those who do help. But when we look at their blank faces and stare into their eyes, we discern cries for help. How, then, do you help these souls who can't understand what you say or even remember your name? You help through your nonanxious presence.

One woman insists on "going home." I know better than to say, "This is your home," to a person with dementia. Without fulfilling her request, I validate it by asking her, "Tell me about your home. Did it have a garden?" A glimmer of recognition comes to her face so I invite her to go outside and see the garden. She grasps several flowers, mutters some incomprehensible words, and forgets about "going home."

I visited a man with profound dementia who rarely spoke, and when he did it was in a whisper. In his room his bony fingers pointed to several pictures of cats on the wall. He mumbled garbled words I couldn't understand. I had no idea if he had painted those cats. Later, the activities director told me he had been a gifted architect and landscaper, who had designed many buildings and parks in Pittsburgh. When he died, the newspapers effusively described his career accomplishments. We never know what genius lies behind the disease we call Alzheimer's.

A social worker told me this story. Every day the husband of a woman with Alzheimer's disease would visit her after his work. She would anticipate his visit and scurry to the door to meet him. One day her husband died of a massive coronary attack. A nursing assistant told his wife that her husband had died. She ran to her room, overcome with grief, and had to be heavily medicated.

For a week the woman repeated the same ritual, obviously forgetting that her husband had died. Each night she relived the shock and had to be sedated. Finally the director of personal care realized what was happening and met the woman at the door. The woman invited her in and offered her cookies. They sat together and watched television. For several weeks, the director continued to distract the woman until the Alzheimer's disease progressed to the point that the woman forgot she had a husband.

As the population of older people with Alzheimer's disease continues to grow, more and more cries for help will emerge. We need to reach across the sea that divides us and offer our hearts in love.

> *Dear Lord, I wonder what it would be like to have Alzheimer's disease, to lose both my mind and identity? If that becomes my experience, do not forget or forsake me. Amen.*

44 SONGS IN THE NIGHT

Read Psalm 98

[People] cry out under a load of oppression; . . .
But no one says, "Where is God my Maker,
   who gives songs in the night."

JOB 35:9-10 (NIV)

After living at Redstone for a year, if you ask me to identify
the highlight of each month, I would have to say the monthly
sing-along with Alzheimer's residents. It all began when Redstone dedicated an organ for use in the worship services, and
I led a sing-along using songs from the 1930s and 1940s. It
was an instant success. The Alzheimer's residents loved it,
and soon independent living residents began to attend. We
even had to move the organ into a larger room to accom-
modate the crowd. Music of the night had won the day!

I intentionally chose songs from bygone years that residents could recall. Most of the residents either sang the lyrics
or mouthed the words. One man, who had sung in a community chorus years ago, sang the first verse of "The Battle
Hymn of the Republic." It may have been the first time he
had soloed in many years, and his singing brought tears to
many eyes. Songs in the night.

A woman, who had been a singer in her past, was lost in
a fog of dementia. One night she burst into song and 1939
was now as she sang "Somewhere Over the Rainbow." A hush
fell over the room. Independent living residents were
astounded that such a magnificent voice could emerge from
the darkness of dementia. Songs in the night.

An elderly British resident asked a man with early Alzheimer's, who formerly had been a tenor soloist, to sing "I'll Take You Home Again, Kathleen." At first the man declined but then agreed. He burst into a beautiful solo, every note perfect, with a resonance in his voice that restored his past. Songs in the night. In all three instances, chords that were silent began to vibrate once more.

The epilogue to the book of Job always bothered me. It seems out-of-step with the story. The "happily-ever-after" ending undercuts the meaning of the book. The truth that Job never loses his integrity when everything is taken from him gets lost in the epilogue. Actually Job keeps his integrity even when disease never leaves his body, when his family is devastated, and when his friends accuse him.

What the book of Job tells me is that when Job found God in the darkness, his questions about the injustices done to him disappear. Job is able to sing "songs in the night," even when the dawn never seems to arrive.

Every month the sing-along reaffirms my faith that God has not abandoned these souls who live in the darkness and the shadow of death. The music, the spirit of love in that room, becomes the presence of God even "under a load of oppression" (35:9, NIV).

What thrilled me was the presence of independent living residents at the sing-along. They had overcome their fears and brought presence to this place. We were at last *the blessed community*, where all are loved and accepted. Some bent to shake the hand or hug dementia residents who had formerly lived independently. Others sat next to dementia residents and helped them follow along with the words.

In this place, located on the far side of the community, where every day is the same and no hope for a cure is in sight, there was a glimpse of hope and joy. Songs pierced the night, and a new day dawned.

Make us aware, O God, that even in the darkest places on earth some love is found and music abounds. Amen.

REFLECTIVE EXERCISES

- Recall situations in your life when you had a fear of strangers. What caused that fear? In what ways do you see these fears in a new light now?

- Reflecting on your life experience, recall some "hidden" angels; persons unknown to you who ministered to you in key moments.

- If you were living in the late 1930s or 1940s what would be your favorite radio shows? songs? movie stars?

- Select one person who is now a soul friend to you. Call or write this friend and relate the qualities you would value in a retirement community.

- If you could choose a person to be your roommate in a nursing home, who would it be?

- It is documented that Thomas Parr, an Englishman, lived until he was 152 years old (1483–1635). He is buried in Westminster Abbey. Physicians claimed that he died "from acute indigestion, from indulging in unnecessary luxuries." How would Mr. Parr fare in modern society? in a retirement community?

HOME AT LAST
End of the Year

The word *home* summons up a place . . . which you have rich and complex feelings about, a place where you feel . . . uniquely at home, which is to say a place where you feel you belong and which in some sense belongs to you.[18]

—FREDERICK BUECHNER

45 LEARNING FROM WISDOM PEOPLE

Read Proverbs 28

Length of days is not what makes age honourable,
nor number of years the true measure of life;
understanding, this is grey hairs,
untarnished life, this is ripe old age.

THE BOOK OF WISDOM 4:8-9 (NJB)

As an older person, I often cringe at some of the cute terms used to describe older people. "Keenagers," "Golden Agers," "Elderberries" leave me cold. The best name for older people I have ever heard originated with the Yoruba tribe in Nigeria. The tribe refers to its older folks as "wisdom people."

It is now over a year since my wife and I moved into this community. What has given us a feeling of home is not only *where* we live but the people with whom we live. Their acceptance has made us feel at home.

Those of us who make up the human race are living longer and longer. There are more than sixty thousand centenarians in America today; in fifty years that number will mushroom and top one million! Healthier diets, regular exercise, and improved medical care have prolonged life for many older people. Scientists even affirm that the natural length of years is one hundred twenty! I can't wait to celebrate the hundredth birthdays of our nonagenarians.

I value the words of Socrates, "There is nothing which for my part I like better . . . than conversing with aged [people]; for I regard them as travellers who have gone a journey which

I too may have to go, and of whom I ought to enquire, whether the way is smooth and easy, or rugged and difficult."

For many years I traveled throughout the country leading workshops on aging. Often I would meet centenarians and would listen to their wisdom. One such wisdom person was Mayme Carpenter. She wrote a book of poetry when she was ninety-nine and titled it, *I'm Ninety-Nine and Doing Fine*, and before her death at one hundred and one, she was working on its sequel, *I'm One Hundred Now, and Fine Anyhow!*

Now I don't have to travel far to encounter the wisdom people who live in this community. Recently, while visiting a friend who is in his nineties, he told me he had subscribed to a new magazine called *Life Extension*. The lead article was "Scientists Seek to Rejuvenate Aging Humans." My friend said, "I might learn something." Another friend who reached his ninetieth year is a computer wizard and gives lessons to other residents who wish to become "computer literate."

One of the most active members of our literary club is a woman in her nineties who reads constantly. Not content to let television devour her time, she is always reading new books and stretching her mind.

After living among these wisdom people for over a year, I have found these qualities in most of them: a positive attitude, a strong will, spiritual beliefs, and a sense of humor. They also love life and live each day to the fullest.

The writer of the Book of Wisdom knew that length of days is not the true measure of graceful aging. Understanding and an untarnished life mark a valued older person.

I count it a blessing to be surrounded here by such wisdom and experience. I consider myself an apprentice in the school of aging, and my mentors are these wisdom people whose experience and wisdom school me for my later years.

God of our weary years,
God of our silent tears,
Thou who hast brought us thus far on the way. . . .
Keep us forever in the path, we pray.

Lines from "Lift Every Voice and Sing," by James Weldon Johnson © Penguin Press. Used by permission.

46 LEARNING TO BE CONTENT

Read Philippians 4:10-14

I have learned to be content with whatever I have.

PHILIPPIANS 4:11

Paul is in a dank Roman prison. His heart's desire of taking the gospel to Spain seems impossible as he spends his days languishing there. Separated from friends and colleagues, he knows his days on this earth are numbered. Yet he writes to the church at Philippi: "I have learned to be content with whatever I have." Paul lives independent of circumstances. He finds peace within himself.

Plenty or poverty makes no difference, nor does the place where he lives. Paul could have complained about his situation. Is prison the reward for his faithful service? Why will God not permit him to take the gospel to Spain? But Paul never gives in to self-pity. He can say, "I can do all things through him who strengthens me." He roots his independence in his dependence on Christ. Stoics were self-sufficient; Paul is Christ-sufficient.

I am learning this contentment. All my life I have been spurred on by a divine discontent, never satisfied with things as they are but dreaming of things that never were. At last in my twilight years, I am at peace. Several months ago I wrote these words in my journal,

> I saw today the first signs of spring. Flowers were springing up everywhere, and I thought of the Zen saying,

"When one flower blooms, it is spring everywhere." It was a harsh, cold winter, creating respiratory problems for me and some confinement to this place. But I am also aware of a new sense of peace, for whatever the winter of my life brings, it will always be spring in my soul.

This is not to say that annoying things won't happen. Bugs in our apartment, trash thrown on our lovely grounds, long waits for service in the dining room, late arrivals of the mail, and problems with the thermostats are constant irritants. But I laugh at most of these annoyances, for "I have learned, in whatsoever state I am, therewith to be content" (Phil.4:11, KJV). Although Paul is referring more to the circumstances in which he found himself rather than his geographical state, I can relate to his words. I had been a Carolinian for over fifty years. I bled Carolina blue. Nothing was finer than to be in Carolina all the time. My wife and I lived in western North Carolina near the mountains; the seasons of the year were all incredible.

I left all that for the new state of Pennsylvania. I became a Steelers fan, put up with weather that has been called "one of the worst in America for respiratory problems." I departed the beauty of the Tar Heel state to live where remnants of the steel and coal industry still mark the environment. But I had learned that I could find peace and contentment despite the circumstances. My blue-and-white North Carolina tee shirt and Davidson hat remain in my closet, faint memories of a past that is history. Now I wear a Pittsburgh basketball shirt and a Steelers hat, reminders of my present.

In the sixth century BCE, the Chinese philosopher Lao Tzu wrote these words,

Without going out my door
I can know all things on earth.
Without looking out of my window
I can know the ways of heaven.
For the further one travels
the less one knows.
The sage therefore arrives without traveling,
sees all without looking.

*God of sacred presence, may I know that contentment is
not found in the place we live but in the person we are.
Amen.*

47 CRUMBLING BUT GROWING

Read 2 Corinthians 4:7-18

> But this precious treasure—this light and power that now shine within us—is held in perishable containers, that is, in our weak bodies. So everyone can see that our glorious power is from God and is not our own. We are pressed on every side by troubles, but we are not crushed and broken. We are perplexed, but we don't give up and quit. . . . We get knocked down, but we get up again and keep going.
>
> 2 CORINTHIANS 4:7-9 (NLT)

A woman visited the studio of the sculptor and artist Michelangelo and watched him hacking away at precious marble. She was obviously unhappy with the growing pile of chips on the floor, considering it a waste. But Michelangelo said, "The more the marble wastes; the more the statue grows."

Paul knew what it meant to have a weak, wasted body. In addition to the physical ailment he mentions in a letter to the Corinthians, he describes his suffering, which included imprisonments, flogging, stoning, shipwreck, and sleepless nights. (See 2 Corinthians 11:23-29.)

Yet Paul affirms that although afflicted, he is not crushed. That same indomitable spirit is ever evident in this retirement community. The years have hacked away at the bodies; time has taken its toll on physical strength. Yet I see evidence of courage and resilience as these residents struggle with these weaknesses of the body.

Kathleen R. Fischer, in her book by the same name, has called such courage grown large in the face of diminishments, "winter grace." It has been a long winter in western Pennsylvania. After suffering from bronchitis in the bitter cold of this winter, I was diagnosed with asthma. I grew worse instead of better, so my allergist suggested I see an ear, nose, and throat specialist. In a matter of weeks, I endured endoscopic sinus surgery that plunged me into a long winter of enforced confinement. The surgery helped, and by May I was feeling much better. I could laugh about my predicament.

What I learned from experience is that when some things are wrung from my life, I need to make peace with myself. I learned neither to yearn after nor to dread their deprivation but seize the moment with the gifts I now have.

I learned how to pace myself and not use my voice unless absolutely necessary. That wasn't easy for someone known for verbosity. But I learned that silence is golden.

During my convalescence, I witnessed members of the community push others in wheelchairs or lend a helping hand to someone on a walker. Even when serious illness or surgery strikes the residents, they rebound with amazing resiliency. These hardy souls call to mind Friedrich Nietzsche's words, "What does not kill me makes me stronger."[19]

When asked the question, "What do you do in a monastery?" a monk replied, "All day long we fall down and get up, fall down and get up again." What a wonderful paradigm for older persons: We get knocked down, but we get up and keep going. As long as this resilience exists and opportunities for service are provided, hope remains. The more the marble wastes; the more the person grows.

Help us, O God, not to be blind to the potentiality of our later years. As our physical nature crumbles, may you keep our inner spirits alive and fruitful. Amen.

48 FINDING A CHURCH HOME

Read Psalm 84

How lovely is your dwelling place,
O Lord of hosts! . . .

. . . .

Even the sparrow finds a home,
    and the swallow a nest for herself, . . .
at your altars, O Lord of hosts,
    my King and my God.
Happy are those who live in your house,
ever singing your praise.

Psalm 84:1, 3-4

For months my wife and I had searched for a new church home. None seemed to meet our needs. Some churches were locked in conflict, while others had a style of worship that did not resonate with our souls. Finally, we ventured to another town not far from us, hoping to find a new church home.

As we entered the sanctuary, the reverence of the congregation impressed us. People in the pews seemed genuinely friendly as they engaged in the ritual of passing the peace. Believe it or not, the minister, Martin Ankrum, spoke about "Finding a Church Home!" How did he know? He based his sermon on the text from Psalm 84, and he talked about the sparrow, that ubiquitous bird that flies everywhere and settles nowhere. (Sounded like our church hopping!) But one sparrow had found a home and built a nest in the sanctuary.

Call it coincidence if you will. My wife and I thought it to be God at work in our lives. We had come to this church at the right time. We had been like the sparrow, flitting from one church to another, until at last we found our resting place. In this church we felt there were no strangers, only friends we had never met.

All of us have an empty place in our heart that is in the shape of God. A faith community is one place where that emptiness can be filled. Since that incredible first Sunday, we have become a part of the congregation. We have joined groups, led groups, and taught Sunday school. We needed a church home, and we found it.

Some residents attend their own church on Sundays. Others ride the van to the church of their choice. Residents in assisted living and others who can't get out attend the Sunday chapel services.

However, we have a growing number of residents who have no church home or have drifted away because their clergy and members have forgotten them. Far too many pastors and priests bypass members in this community, claiming they are too busy with the needs of the parish. However, no one needs the church and pastoral ministry more than older people, regardless of where they are.

My wife and I have been blessed by the ministry of First Presbyterian Church, Greensburg, Pennsylvania, and others here have had their spiritual needs met by other congregations. We may be a faith community in this place, but that does not mean the residents have to give up a vital connection to the churches in their communities.

I find it intriguing that worship with Alzheimer's residents always involves the request to sing "Little Brown Church in the Vale." No place was so dear to their childhood.

Why, then, should their home churches forsake them? People here are God's oldest friends. We have found a church home, but many of God's friends are homeless.

Parent God, you have placed the solitary in families and church is your family of faith. Yes, we can find you in our moments of solitude and contemplation, but we need the support, presence, and love of a faith community. Amen.

49 SEEKING THE WELFARE OF THE COMMUNITY

Read Jeremiah 29:1-14

> Seek the welfare of the city where I have sent you into exile, and pray to the LORD on its behalf, for in its welfare you will find your welfare. . . .
>
> For surely I know the plans I have for you, says the LORD, plans for your welfare and not for harm, to give you a future with hope.
>
> JEREMIAH 29:7, 11

Jeremiah writes a letter to the exiles in Babylon and tells them to entertain no false hopes for a speedy return to their homeland. They are to seek the welfare of the city where they live, for its welfare will contribute to their own. And he adds that God has plans for their welfare and a future with hope.

Although I now felt settled in the retirement community, something was missing. It took a while before it dawned on me that I lacked involvement in the larger community. I had been so insulated by life in the retirement community that I played no role in the welfare of the larger community. But interesting circumstances transpired to change that.

One of my best friends in the retirement community was Bill Kunkle. Although only a few months from reaching the ripe old age of ninety, he modeled creative retirement. He had forged a new career after his retirement and devoted himself to work for the welfare of the community. We often shared our mutual love of libraries, and Bill had been the major player in bringing a new library to the community.

On several occasions he shared his vision of the new library and challenged me to form a Friends of the Library group.

One morning Bill and I were leading the daily devotional over our closed-circuit television when he suffered a massive stroke. Three days later he died. Like Moses, he saw the fulfillment of his dream for a new library only from afar. But he left a legacy for all who followed him, and I took up the task of making Bill's dream a reality.

Two months after Bill's death, the Friends of the Library held its organizational meeting in our retirement community, and residents were encouraged to volunteer. Many seemed interested in reading to children or offering their computer skills to teach others.

The vision of Bill Kunkle, a man I had only known for a year, was coming to fruition. Our energized group of volunteers worked hard to bring about community involvement. As I became involved in the Friends of the Library as its new president, I now found myself engaged in the welfare of the community. The final piece of my volunteer work fell into place. I walked the streets of the town and realized that although I initially thought myself an exile in a strange land, now I began to feel at home in the larger community.

One day as I left the old library, church bells were pealing the music of a hymn. I stopped to listen to "Praise Ye the Lord, the Almighty." My heart heard some of its words, which became God's word to me.

> Hast thou not seen
> How thy desires e'er have been
> Granted in what He ordaineth?

The welfare of the city had become my own welfare!

O Christ, who walked the roads of life in Galilee and trod the city's streets, we thank you for opportunities to give back to the world some of the gifts given to us. Amen.

50 WHEN PRAYER IS ANSWERED

Read Jeremiah 29:1-14

For surely I know the plans I have for you, says the LORD, plans for your welfare and not for harm, to give you a future with hope. . . . When you search for me, you will find me; if you seek me with all your heart.

—JEREMIAH 29:11, 13

Like the exiles in Babylon, I often felt a stranger and wondered how I would ever fit into this new community. I prayed about it and often remembered God's word to the exiles: that God would give them a future with hope.

I believed God had led my wife and me to make this our home for the later years. Many retirement communities were beyond our means. Neither of us wanted to burden our families or live with them as a "fifth wheel." Furthermore, my own family health history indicates that my wife might at some time be burdened with my care. In parish ministry I had seen far too many caregivers collapse under that stress and become victims of their own care for loved ones.

God had plans for our welfare, to lead us to this community, which was affordable. Furthermore, Redstone had a benevolent care fund that would provide support if we outlived our assets. The fund would assure that we could live on campus and receive needed services regardless of our ability to pay. We knew that if and when we needed health care, it would be forthcoming. So we took the step that will assure continuing care for our remaining years.

God answered my prayers for a "future with hope" by placing me in a community that affords ministry opportunities every day. In this place of human need, I do not have to set aside all my training and experience. Not a day passes that someone doesn't need assistance. God did have plans for our welfare in our later years. While struggling with this major life transition, I had no earthly idea what moving to this community would be like. Now, more than a year later, I know it was God's plan for my welfare.

For years I have worked in the field of aging and retirement. I have counseled with many older people and their adult children about the later years of life. I always point to options that will bring fulfillment and joy to all concerned. I confess my bias now. Affordable retirement communities with a continuum of care may well be the best answer, not only for those of my civic generation but for the surging population of baby boomers. Happiness and fulfillment are found in these communities.

Great Mystery of our universe, we thank you for hearing our heartfelt prayer. We give you thanks for leading us to this home. May we live gratefully and graciously in all our coming years. Amen.

51 HOME AT LAST

Read Hebrews 11:13-16

They confessed that they were strangers and foreigners on the earth, for people who speak in this way make it clear that they are seeking a homeland. . . . They desire a better country, that is, a heavenly one.

HEBREWS 11:13-14, 16

Several months ago my wife and I returned to North Carolina, where I spoke at the tenth anniversary of a retirement community. During time for dialogue, a gentleman said, "I used to call my place an apartment. Now I call it my home." I admit at that moment I did not have similar feelings. Everything was still strange and new and being in North Carolina again touched off a lot of nostalgia and regrets.

It is now a year later, and this community has become "home." As a minister, I lived in eleven somewhat permanent domiciles. When I retired, I felt that Morganton would be my final staying place. But when you get settled in, unexpected changes happen.

Some people claim that going into retirement communities makes us "displaced persons," with no clear membership in community life and its responsibilities, no close neighbors or friends. I beg to differ. We have many friends in this community, and now our lives are becoming entwined with the larger community.

One song the residents in assisted living love to sing is the 1928 song "Show Me the Way to Go Home." In my first months here that song would have kicked up nostalgic feelings about my home in North Carolina. But now, Redstone is my home; this staff and these residents are my family. Whenever I go somewhere and return to *my apartment here*, I sing "Show Me the Way to Go Home," for this is now my home.

Like those ancient believers addressed in Hebrews, we all seek ultimately a heavenly city, whose builder and maker is God. God has prepared that final home, which Jesus promised to all believers. But until that time comes, this is home.

I have long believed that home does not depend on the neighborhood or the size of the house or people who are your neighbors. Home is a place of refuge, reliability, and stability. When we are at home, we know it.

All my life I have been a wanderer, a pilgrim seeking a better country. I am not alone in this feeling. Theologian Paul Tillich has stated, "In the certainty of the omnipresent God, we are always at home, and not at home, rooted and uprooted, resting and wandering, being placed and displaced, known by one place and not known by any place."[20] I have those same ambivalent feelings. My true home is not on this earth, and I will always feel a displaced person here. Yet I rejoice that God has called me to a retirement home that affords a measure of security and wholeness until life's end.

Recently, as spring burst forth with its incredible beauty, I was taking a solitary walk around the place when Richard, another resident, joined me. We chatted for a while, and he seemed "at home." Then I walked on, staring at the blue sky and drifting clouds, it felt good to be here. Memories of former homes now vaguely recur only in scattered dreams. God has indeed led us to this home. The words of a hymn by Horatius Bonar came to mind and became my prayer:

I heard the voice of Jesus say,
"I am this dark world's Light;
Look unto Me, thy morn shall rise,
And all thy day be bright."
I looked to Jesus, and I found
In Him my Star, my Sun;
And in that Light of life I'll walk,
Till traveling days are done.

52 SETTLING IN . . . AT LAST

Read Philippians 4:8-9

Finally, beloved, whatever is true, whatever is honorable,
whatever is just, whatever is pure, whatever is pleasing,
whatever is commendable, if there is any excellence and
if there is anything worthy of praise, think about these
things.

PHILIPPIANS 4:8

It has been a year since we first moved into this retirement
community. My attitude has changed completely since those
early days. Recently, a new resident seemed lost and bewil-
dered and asked, "Will I ever settle in?" I replied, "It takes
time and a lot of prayer."

I first titled this book *Has My Life Come to This?* as I
worked through the difficult transition from my former community, where I had invested so much of my life. I wondered
if the strangeness of this community would ever dissipate.

Then I began to realize that life here was good, and I could
make this my home. I recalled the story I had heard of the
famous sculptor, engraver, and painter, Hubert von Herkomer. When his aged father, a wood chopper, could no
longer live by himself, his son took him into his own home
and took care of him.

Von Herkomer's father loved to work with clay, but his
hands were so crippled by arthritis that his efforts usually
failed. One night he climbed the stairs to his room, a dejected
old man. His son, aware of the situation, worked all night

with the misshapen clay until a beautiful sculpture emerged. When the old man came down the stairs for breakfast, the morning's ray shone on the sculpture. The old man gasped and exclaimed, "Why it's better than I thought!" So, the second title of the book was *It's Better Than I Thought*.

As time passed, I began to settle in and realize this is my home. I have seen the seasons come and go. The first summer was a time of great excitement and anticipation as I began to settle in and to explore this new community.

I have always loved the autumn of the year with its brilliant tapestry of colors and falling leaves. During that first fall, I began to realize that life was better than I thought in this community.

Then winter arrived with its blustery winds and zero weather. It was a minor setback, aggravated by serious respiratory problems, asthma, and sinus surgery. But I discovered that this was not only a caring community but a good place to be when adversity comes.

Then spring dawned, and new hope emerged as God's world once again came to new life. With it came my realization that I was where God wanted me to be. The words of William Cowper's hymn exemplified my own experience:

> Sometimes a light surprises
> The Christian while he sings;
> It is the Lord, who rises
> With healing in his wings:
> When comforts are declining,
> He grants the soul again
> A season of clear shining,
> To cheer it after rain.

God had surprised me with a "a season of clear shining." My spiritual journey has taken me through many seasons of the soul. Now, in this final transition of life to a retirement community, I have settled in and feel at home. Here I will dwell until traveling days are done.

Two sisters, former Baptist missionaries, lived together in a nursing home until the day one sister died. When the other sister heard the news, she told her friends, "I sure hope sister gets settled in!" I am sure that when the day comes, God will surprise me with wonders I never dreamed could exist. Then this temporary life will end, and there will be a room in the Father's house. I will settle into that home, where all is light and unspeakable beauty.

Wonderful God, help us to realize that you go before us and with us and make any place a home. Amen.

REFLECTIVE EXERCISES

- Recall the houses where you have lived in your lifetime. Which one of them felt like home? Why?

- What kinds of ministry could community churches provide for people in retirement communities who do not drive?

- Today's retirees are considerably more demanding than their predecessors. What demands will they make on retirement communities?

- A recent newsletter on retirement living states, "The new generation is looking more for two-bedroom continuing care retirement communities with at least 1,500-square feet, a washer and dryer, and some custom features." What does this mean for future planners? In what ways might these physical amenities give retirees a sense of home?

- Reflecting on your life, recall those moments of difficult transition that you later realized were "better than you thought."

NOTES

1. Robert Browning, "Rabbi Ben Ezra," *The Columbia Granger's World of Poetry* (New York: Columbia University Press, 1995).

2. John C. Morgan, ed., *Awakening the Soul: A Book of Daily Devotions* (Boston, Mass.: Skinner House Books, 2001), Feb. 5.

3. Frank Henderson MacEowen, T*he Mist-Filled Path: Celtic Wisdom for Exiles, Wanderers, and Seekers* (Novato, Calif.: New World Library, 2002), xxi.

4. Paul Tournier, *A Place for You: Psychology and Religion* (New York: Harper & Row, 1968), 162.

5. John Greenleaf Whittier, "Dear Lord and Father of Mankind," *The United Methodist Hymnal* (Nashville, Tenn.: United Methodist Publishing House, 1989), no. 358.

6. Richard Lyon Morgan, *Fire in the Soul: A Prayer Book for the Later Years* (Nashville, Tenn.: Upper Room Books, 2000), 106–7.

7. Joan D. Chittister, *Scarred by Struggle, Transformed by Hope* (Grand Rapids, Mich.: Wm. B. Eerdmans Publishing Co., 2003), 38.

8. Paul Wilkes, *Beyond the Walls: Monastic Wisdom for Everyday Life* (New York: Image Books, 2000), 121.

9. John O'Donohue, *Eternal Echoes: Celtic Reflections on Our Yearning to Belong* (New York: HarperCollins Publishers, 1999), 258.

10. Robert Benson, *The Body Broken: Answering God's Call to Love One Another* (New York: Doubleday, 2003), 125.

11. Edwin Markham, "OutWitted," in A. L. Alexander, ed., *Poems That Touch the Heart* (New York: Doubleday, 1956), 403.

12. MacEowen, *The Mist-Filled Path*, xxii.

13. Jane Marie Thibault, *A Deepening Love Affair: The Gift of God in Later Life* (Nashville, Tenn.: Upper Room Books, 1993), 192–93.

14. Fred Rogers, *The World According to Mr. Rogers: Important Things to Remember* (New York: Hyperion, 2003), 188.

15. Anna B. Warner, "Jesus Loves Me," *United Methodist Hymnal*, no. 191.

16. John O'Donohue, *Anam Cara: A Book of Celtic Wisdom* (New York: HarperCollins Publishers, 1997), 14.

17. Ibid., 12.

18. Frederick Buechner, *The Longing for Home: Recollections and Reflections* (New York: HarperCollins Publisher, 1996), 7.

19. Friedrich Nietzsche, *Twilight of the Idols and the Anti-Christ*, trans. R. J. Hollingdale Jr. (New York: Penguin Books, 1969), 120.

20. Paul Tillich, *Systematic Theology*, vol. 1 (Chicago: University of Chicago Press, 1955), 308.

BIBLICAL INDEX

ABOUT THE AUTHOR

RICHARD L. MORGAN is a retired Presbyterian minister and has served as chaplain in hospitals, retirement communities, and nursing homes. He and his wife, Alice Ann Morgan, reside at Redstone Highlands retirement community in Pennsylvania, where he does volunteer work in pastoral care with Alzheimer's and other dementia residents. He and his wife have led workshops on retirement living in many retirement communities. He is the author of many books on the spirituality of aging, published by Upper Room Books.